Japanese Stone Gardens

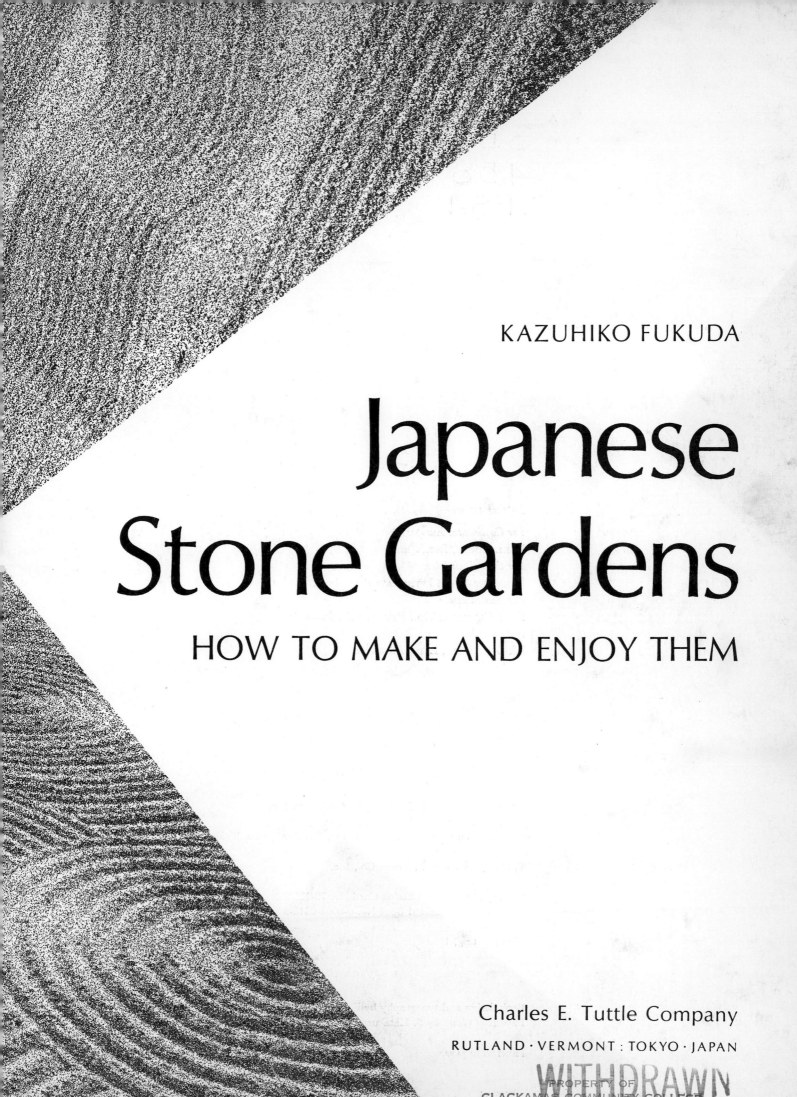

KAZUHIKO FUKUDA

Japanese Stone Gardens

HOW TO MAKE AND ENJOY THEM

Charles E. Tuttle Company

RUTLAND · VERMONT : TOKYO · JAPAN

Representatives

For Continental Europe:
BOXERBOOKS, INC., *Zurich*
For the British Isles:
PRENTICE-HALL INTERNATIONAL, INC., *London*
For Australasia:
PAUL FLESCH & CO., PTY. LTD., *Melbourne*
For Canada:
M. G. HURTIG, LTD., *Edmonton*

Published by the Charles E. Tuttle Company, Inc.
of Rutland, Vermont & Tokyo, Japan
with editorial offices at Suido 1-chome, 2-6, Bunkyo-ku, Tokyo

© 1970 by Charles E. Tuttle Co., Inc.

Library of Congress Catalog Card No. 73-125562
International Standard Book No. 0-8048-0318-8

First printing, 1970

Book design and typography by F. Sakade
Layout of plates by S. Katakura

PRINTED IN JAPAN

Table of Contents

18603

PLATES IN COLOR

1. Sampo-in, Daikaku-ji, Kyoto   *41*
2. Shoden-ji, Kyoto   *113*
3. Tofuku-ji, Kyoto   *159*
4. Raikyu-ji, Takahashi, Okayama Pref.   *239*

TABLES

1. Rock Selection   210
2. Ratio of Rockwork to Garden Area   216

■ Foreword

by Taro Okamoto

MANY PEOPLE misunderstand the Japanese aesthetic. They think it is represented only by copies of Chinese models—which have greatly influenced Japan since the Nara period (710–788)—by the faces in colored woodblock prints *(ukiyo-e)* which flourished at the end of the Tokugawa era (1603–1867), or else as characterized by quiet taste *(wabi)* and elegant simplicity *(shibumi)*. In fact the Japanese aesthetic is not confined to such a narrow framework; it is more liberal, philosophical, and bold, confronting space with exuberant vitality.

Classical stone gardens present striking examples of Japanese qualities. It is in these gardens that I feel the nation's spirit most strongly, not in the "exquisite" workmanship of Japanese art. Gardens modeled after nature, the mysterious feeling produced by *karesansui,* the appearance of rocks rushing upon us in everlasting silence, and the profound thoughts and unique view of the world shaped there—the unfathomable qualities of all these provide mankind with important subjects for study and contemplation.

It is my great pleasure to write the Foreword to this book since the author, Kazuhiko Fukuda, successfully presents the distinctive features of these Japanese gardens through his excellent photography and circumspect description.

TARO Ok____.

■ Introduction

GARDENS can be classified into two basic styles. One is the geometric, in which the garden is arranged in a formal and symmetrical style; the other is the landscape garden style, in which a natural landscape is copied to present the essence of nature. The former is found mostly in Europe and is represented by the gardens at Versailles, while the latter is typified by the Chinese or Japanese garden.

Among landscape gardens there are those that have ponds, springs, and fountains, and those that use no water, as is the case with Japanese stone gardens. These dry landscape gardens *(karesansui)* best represent the unique beauty of the Japanese landscaping tradition. Although karesansui came to include moss and plantings, they originally possessed only rocks and stones arranged to depict a natural landscape, the resting place of Buddha, or the world of Taoist demigod-hermits. Although stones were used as fetishes by many ancient peoples, nowhere but in Japan have they so widely and concretely served as religious icons, sometimes being worshiped as gods themselves. This indicates the national belief in animism, as the people's hopes for eternal life were entrusted to the unchangeable stones. Thus the stones worked their charm and were metamorphosed into the forms of mountains, Buddhas, and lesser gods.

Japanese culture developed under the influence of China, and its civilization took root in Chinese ground. Stone gardens originated in imitation of the Chinese karesansui of the T'ang and Sung periods (7th to 12th centuries) for the homes of imperial nobles, retreats of painters and men of letters, and hermitages of Buddhist priests. The stone garden styles called *sekko* (a small stone garden up to six by nine feet in area) and *kazan* (miniature mountains, a garden built with rocks depicting mountains) bristled with piles of gigantic, fantastically shaped rocks. The introduction of stone gardens for Japanese temple yards came when Zen Buddhism was brought to Japan from China in the Kamakura period (13th century).

The Chinese karesansui of the T'ang and Sung periods express a different feeling from those of Japan. They seem to imply an attitude of reverence for the stones, which are appreciated for their monstrous or supernatural forms. Thus the aim of the Chinese stone garden was to inspire awareness of nature's beautiful molding through water, wind, and weather. By contrast the attitude implicit in the Japanese variety is both more religious and naturalistic. For example, one attached to a temple expresses the world view of Zen, and the appreciative viewer discovers the figures of Buddha in the stones; thus its significance is not visual as the re-creation of a scenic landscape in miniature but as a place where hearts can commune with one another, and where the spirit is directed more certainly toward the enlightenment it seeks. In the words of the French architect Le Corbusier, the garden "is the stage of a mystery drama." The idea of forming the figures of a crane and a turtle (traditional Japanese symbols of longevity) or representing the world of Taoist demigod-hermits indicates that the Japanese regarded these stones as immutable and prayed to them for the happiness and prosperity of their families. Thus the form and substance of these stone gardens are quite different from those of Chinese or European gardens. The Japanese religious sense and feeling for life permeate them, and it is difficult to understand karesansui in depth without reflecting on the mystical implications of Buddhism.

This book is divided into two parts. Part One introduces the *shoin* and *sado* styles, explaining their beauty and the mystical implications of their content and, in so doing, instructs the reader in the knowledge necessary for full appreciation of these gardens. The *shoin*-style garden is constructed facing a living room of a residence or a temple. It exists to be looked at and appreciated as a work of art, for it is a highly creative aesthetic expression that can be compared to other concrete art forms. Part Two gives instruction on each step in the making of the garden, from the selection of rocks through the garden's maintenance.

The appropriate mental attitude for the creation of a karesansui requires that one find symbols in the forms of natural stones, creating with them a beautiful scene that will comfort man's soul with the tranquillity produced by aesthetic stillness. To understand dry landscape gardening one must feel that the stones are living things, like trees and shrubs. The beauty of the garden is individual and differs from all others according to the nature and shape of the stones, which are selected for their natural qualities; each stone possesses beauty of edges and lines, the vigor of which is respected. This force emerges when well-arranged adjacent stones confront one another and the beauty of the arrangement becomes evident: the design consists only of the static energy implied by the relationship of the stones.

The design for a stone garden may be found by closely observing natural scenery. For example, one might study the scenic beauty of the stones in a coastal region or a natural field. Regarding the actual composition of the garden rockwork, reference to the distinguished classical gardens presented here will offer valuable suggestions. Making a fine stone garden requires, above all else, the study of as many examples as possible in order to train the eye. This book is intended for those interested in gardens and who have few opportunities to see actual karesansui. It is hoped that the reader will come to appreciate and understand the artistry of these gardens so that he may build a stone garden in the

Japanese style for himself. In this volume, therefore, I have recorded all the noted Japanese stone gardens which I have studied and photographed over the past ten years, including photographs, sketches, and garden plans as reference data on the practical aspects of stone gardening.

I would like to express my appreciation to the owners of the various gardens who gave their permission for the photographs to appear in this book. The figures were borrowed from the library of the Tokyo College of Agriculture; the surveys were supplied through the kindness of Messrs. Osami Mori, Mirei Shigemori, and the faculty of the Agriculture Department of the University of Kyoto.

It is my sincere hope that this book will be helpful to those interested in the beauty of Japanese stone gardens and useful to those who intend to build them.

—KAZUHIKO FUKUDA

PART ONE

·

Classical
Stone Gardens

1 : Landscape Gardens

KAZAN ROCKWORK

Plates (4), 10, 11 *Kazan* is a style of dry landscape gardening in which a panorama of mountains or a mountain range is depicted by rockwork. Literally meaning "miniature mountains," *kazan* was originally a garden style of the Sui period in China (6th century) and was introduced to Japan in the Kamakura period (13th century), where it was composed as a magnificent mountain view in a garden. In this style forms of mountains are represented in a small space by an arrangement of rocks, and miniature mountains are composed by standing gigantic rocks close together or piling them up in a certain way. Sometimes only one rock is used to depict the mountain scenery. Accordingly, mountainlike stones are the principal material of the *kazan* style. Various shapes of stones are appreciated as representing certain mountains.

Saiho-ji

Plates 1–3 ■ The Saiho-ji garden is noted for possessing Japan's oldest existing
Figure 1 *kazan* rockwork. Zen Buddhist monks formerly sat among the miniature mountains and disciplined themselves, striving for enlightenment and a true understanding of Zen. The rockwork represents the innermost mountain recesses and ravines where a noted Chinese Zen priest lived in seclusion. The garden was constructed in Kyoto during the 13th century. Its area is 9,146 square feet.

Toko-ji and Ginkaku-ji

Plates 4–6 ■ The rockwork in the Toko-ji and Ginkaku-ji gardens seems magnifi-
Figure 2 cent and supernatural in striking contrast to that at Saiho-ji. Bristling, gigantic rocks express craggy mountain cliffs, and the design of both demonstrates the strong influence of the Chinese *kazan* style. The Toko-ji garden was constructed in the 13th century in Kofu, Yamanashi Prefecture, and has an area of 15,979 square feet. The Ginkaku-ji garden, in Kyoto, dates from the 15th century; its area is 1,080 square feet.

FIG. 1. Saiho-ji stone garden. (Saiho-ji, Kyoto)

FIG. 2. Ungo-an garden. This garden merits
attention because its kazan rockwork is the
same as that of the Toko-ji garden. (No longer
existent)

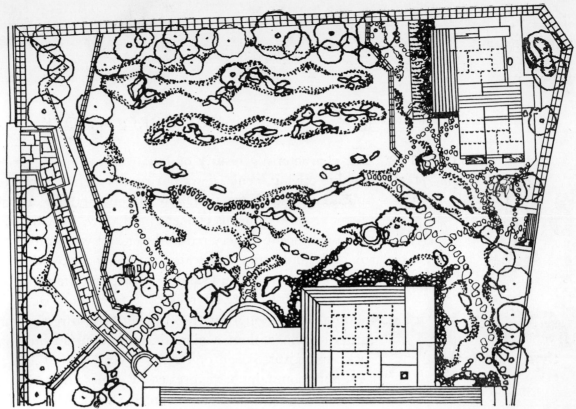

FIG. 3. Garden plan. (Ogawa residence, Masuda, Shimane Pref.)

Joei-ji

Plates 7–9 ■ This rockwork depicts eight scenic mountains in China, each rock representing a majestic mountain. The garden expresses a more magnanimous or universal world view than that commonly associated with *kazan,* for it is thought that the opportunity to contemplate the mountain scenery of the vast Chinese continent at one's feet will spur the cultivation of a generous spirit. The garden is in Yamaguchi Prefecture and is said to have been constructed by Sesshu, the noted 15th-century Zen priest-painter. Its area is 8,608 square feet.

Ogawa Residence

Plates 12–17 ■ This magnificent rockwork depicts the mountain ranges of western
Figure 3 Japan. A sea of white sand surrounds the land masses of the three-range mossy earth heaps, and the rock groups standing on the moss represent the forms of steep mountain ranges. This garden is the largest and most excellent in composition of all the dry landscape gardens depicting mountain ranges with *kazan* rockwork. As the illustrations show, the garden path runs across the stone bridge to the steppingstones on the mossy mounds adjacent to the house. The viewer's attention is thus directed to the scenery of the opposite mountains while he is walking along one range. The mossy earth heaps are in the sandbank pattern, their curved contours expressing the beautiful pattern of a seashore. The garden was designed in 1959 by Mirei Shigemori, who stands foremost among contemporary Japanese landscape architects, and shows well his outstanding skill in garden design. It is located in Masuda, Shimane Prefecture, and has an area of 14,203 square feet.

SHUKKEI ROCKWORK

Plates (18), 69–72
Figures 4–16,
26, 27

The characteristic beauty of Japanese gardens is never derived from simply copying scenic views but results rather from idealization, symbolization, and abstraction, wherein one finds beauty of condensed expression. *Shukkei* means concentrated view, in which the garden-lover sees magnificent scenery reduced to a size within his grasp. In karesansui, such landscapes are created with only rockwork and plants. *Shukkei* rockwork uses rocks and sand to depict mountains, valleys, rivers, seas, and lakes, just as *kazan* rockwork represents steep and precipitous mountains. No longer is the copying of nature the garden's aim, but rather symbolization: a gigantic mountain is symbolized by a single rock, and a vast ocean or rushing river by sand and pebbles. Water, seas, and mountains are expressed by stones and sand alone, and a deep forest by a single plant or trimmed shrub. This symbolization is the aesthetic device of the karesansui and is essential to its appreciation and construction, for without symbolization and abstraction it is impossible to create one of true beauty.

The dry waterfall *(karataki)* in a *shukkei* is composed of smaller rockworks. A rock called *taki-ishi,* with a vertically streaked surface, is used to simulate the waterfall. At each side of it stand attendant rocks in a waterfall *(takizoe-ishi* or *wakiji-ishi);* they also have vertical striping. Their height is supposed to be less than half that of the waterfall rock, as these three form a trinity. If one were to draw lines from the outside bottom of the attendant stones to the top of the *taki-ishi,* an equilateral triangle would result. A *karataki* rockwork is always composed on the east side of the garden because a stream is sure to flow from east to west. To so construct a waterfall is identical with erecting a shrine facing the east, for a waterfall is regarded as the holiest place in the Orient, particularly in Japan.

Stone bridges are constructed in various forms in accordance with the scenes that the *shukkei* rockwork depicts. The material used is a key to the scenery. Thus a naturally flat stone is used over steep and dark valleys in the upper stream; artificially cut stones are used in the lower reaches, and earthen bridges over rivers in open fields. Boards are used for temporary bridges over clear streams in fields so that the owner of the garden can change them when necessary because of weathering, or because he wants to change the mood of the garden by using a different kind of board. Natural- or cut-stone bridges are usually accompanied by attendant rocks *(hashizoe-ishi)* on the sides of both ends. These stones give emphasis to the bridge and the boundaries between it and the banks, drawing the viewer's attention to its decorative quality. *Hashizoe-ishi* are in all cases adjuncts to the stone bridge, and very large or conspicuous stones are never used in these places.

FIG. 4. Daisen-in garden: 1) kei-seki, an islet; 2) karataki rockwork, a natural stone grooved vertically with a surface that appears as though water were actually falling down it (Plate 18); 3 and 4) kei-seki, a deep valley; 5) white sand stream flowing from the karataki; 6) stone bridge, one aspect of the deep mountain valley symbolized by a natural stone slab; 7) decorative stones beside the stone bridge; 8–10) kei-seki, mountains, capes, and islets; 11) jinko-seki, an incense stone; 12) kei-seki, 13) funa-ishi, a fishing boat afloat; 14) kei-seki, a mountain peak; 15) enzan-seki, a distant mountain; 16) kei-seki, a landscape of fields. (Daisen-in, Daitoku-ji, Kyoto)

Kei-seki is a stone or stone arrangement which depicts in condensed version the scenery of a mountain, an islet, or a shore. It is very symbolically treated. Occasionally dry landscape gardens are composed only with *kei-seki*. *Enzan-seki* is a triangular stone or stone arrangement representing the shape of a noted mountain, copied as though it were viewed from a distance. Gardens in *shukkei* built by collecting and condensing various scenes or landscapes formed of such stones are called *kazan-jukei*. Uncommon rocks of high value *(mei-seki)* are sometimes used for *kei-seki*. They are outstanding in shape, texture, and quality and because of their scarcity value command prices equal to those paid for contemporary industrial works of art. However, a garden composed of these rocks is dilettantish in character and is not highly regarded or appreciated in karesansui design.

Streams in dry landscape gardens are expressed in different ways according to the nature of each *shukkei,* as in Figure 5. Split stones, chestnut-colored stones, crushed pebbles, and other stones are used upstream, with the pebbles expressing the aspect of a deep stream replete with limpid pools. White sand expresses a large, flat body of water, such as sea, or a large river in a plain. A small lake is depicted by crushed pebbles, a large one usually by sand or gravel. The beauty of streams in stone gardening lies in their expression of water by means of stones and sand.

FIG. 5. Myoshin-ji garden and detached building. The karesansui is arranged in the back on the left. It depicts water falling down the rocks in several tiers into the big river in front. All the stones for the bridges were artificially cut. The white sand in front describes an expansive river where islets seem to float and points of land seem to push out. A path of steppingstones runs throughout the garden to enable the viewer to appreciate it well. (No longer existent)

FIG. 7. Detail of kei-seki and enzan-seki in the Myoshin-ji garden. Stones around the spring suggest steep mountains and dark valleys. The white sand is spread to represent the shallows around the stone lantern in the rear. Crushed pebbles are scattered like rough sand in the front part to give variety to the stream. The stone bridges are constructed in such a way that those who wish to walk through may appreciate the beauty of the scenery from all directions. The large trees are pine and the trimmed shrubs are azaleas. This garden is regarded as one of the best examples of composite scenic beauty of the shukkei style. (No longer existent)

FIG. 6. Detail of Myoshin-ji garden. The split stones for the stream bed indicate its quiet nature and great depth. The boat-shaped stone under the stone bridge on the right expresses the repose of the stream. The drum-shaped wooden bridge on the left is called a taiko-bashi and is for decorative effect to express the feeling of being in an enchanted garden. (No longer existent)

7

FIG. 8. Example of a small shukkei. The dry waterfall is on the right, and the natural stone bridge is seen in the center. A large boat-shaped stone is positioned on the crushed pebbles depicting water.

FIG. 9. Typical example of shukkei. The karataki rockwork and natural stone bridge are seen upstream. Rocks depicting mountains on the lower stream represent the scenic beauty of the valley. Downstream on the left a small lake is symbolized.

FIG. 10. Variation of the garden style of Myoshin-ji (Fig. 5).

FIG. 11. Spacious lake of white sand at Myoshin-ji. Steep mountains of the kei-seki and enzan-seki arrangement stand on the left shore. The cut-stone bridge connects the islets, where pine and maple trees are planted. This beautiful combination of plants gives an interesting color effect in the fall, with tinted leaves of maple among the green of pine needles. (No longer existent)

FIG. 12. Variation of the Myoshin-ji garden style. The dry waterfall below the stone lantern and the natural stone bridge near the basin are beautifully arranged. Turning to the left, the stream flows under a second bridge of natural stone and becomes a large river. The kazan rockwork on the left represents rugged mountain scenery in miniature. Arranged stones here and there on the bank are kei-seki and enzan-seki, which indicate that this is a garden of collected landscapes.

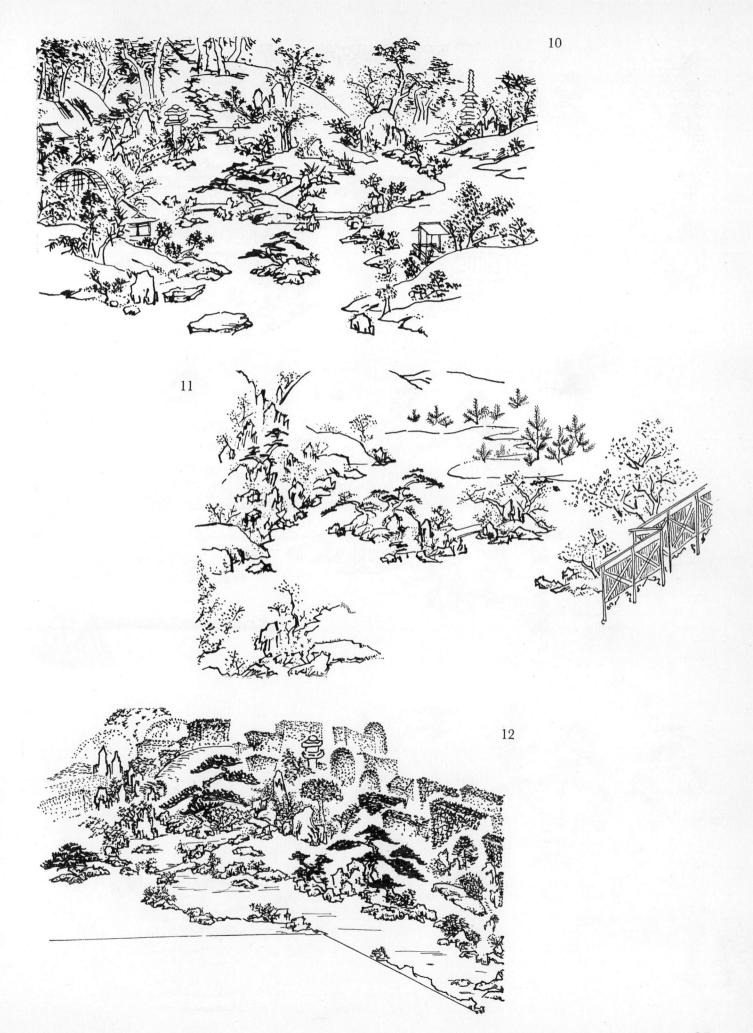

10

11

12

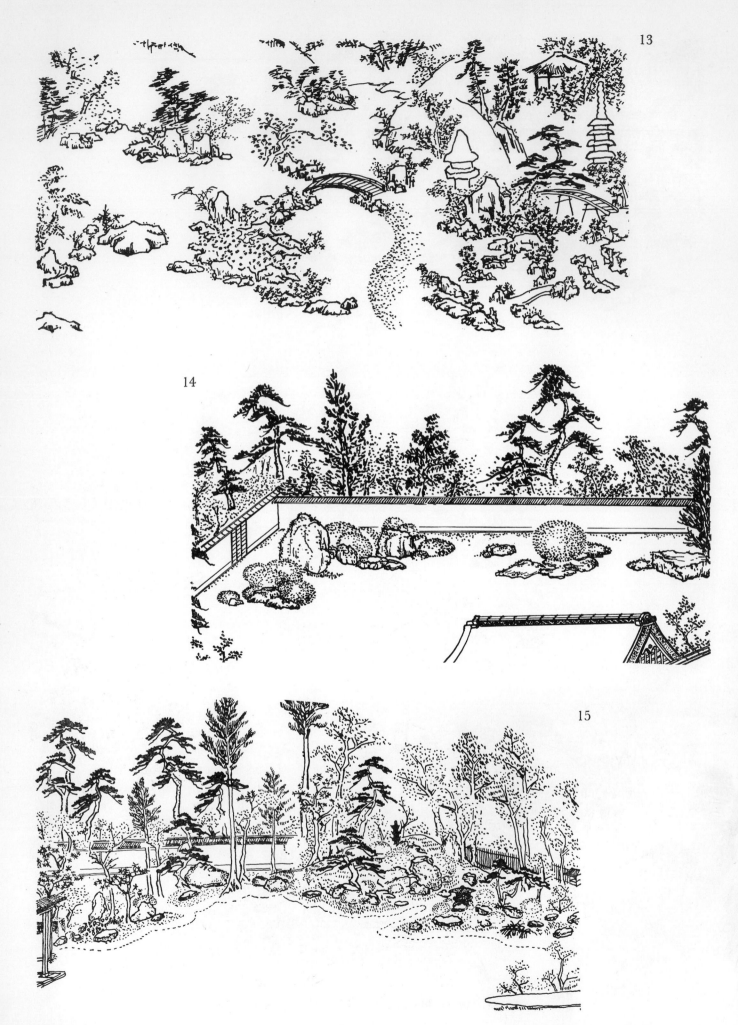

FIG. 13. Typical dry landscape garden of collected landscapes. This garden has an unusually wide visual field. The arrangement is similar to a large map: a wooden board bridge in the center, a lake, distant and miniature mountains, a karataki (at the foot of the lantern), and several valleys are placed within a vast landscape.

FIG. 14. Temple buildings and garden. This garden represents a landscape in miniature using only kei-seki and roundly trimmed azaleas, the latter depicting fields, on white sand. It is a magnificently concentrated landscape. (No longer existent)

FIG. 15. Shukkei with mountains in the corner. Kei-seki and enzan-seki are seen at the foot of the mountains. The foreground is covered with white sand representing a sea. A grand landscape is here composed. (No longer existent)

FIG. 16. Residential garden. Scarcely any arrangement of rocks can be seen here. Trimmed azaleas fill much of the space and encircle the earthen bridge at the center. The view from the bridge is of the trimmed shrubs, which look as though they were mountains robed in their finest green. In May, however, the garden will be painted in hues of crimson, pink, and white. The startling beauty of color-contrast, as the azaleas are reflected on the white sand, can only be seen in karesansui. (No longer existent)

FIG. 17. Daisen-in garden. All the rocks and stones are of hard quality and were gathered from mountains. The surfaces have weathered but are bright in various dark hues. (Daisen-in, Daitoku-ji, Kyoto)

Daisen-in

Plates 18–30
Figures 17, 18

■ This garden is the oldest in the *shukkei* style. Rozan, a noted scenic mountain in China, is here re-created in miniature. The white sand flows down the three-level rocks and seems to gush under the bridge into a large, calm river. Around the upper stream stones are arranged to depict steep mountains, and in the area around the lower stream a tranquil landscape is presented. The composition resembles that of Japanese *sumi-e* (a black-and-white ink painting of a landscape) and adapts the effective *san-en* technique to landscape design. *San-en* is a term meaning three distant landscapes, according to the medieval artistic theory of China. These are: 1) a mountaintop landscape, 2) a mountainous landscape with views both forward and backward, and 3) a landscape with hills in the foreground. In this garden they are: 1) the gigantic *karataki* rockwork, 2) the triangular rocks depicting noted distant mountains and other mountain-shaped rocks of the upper stream, and 3) the even *enzan-seki* rockwork of the lower stream. The garden is in Kyoto and was constructed during the 15th century. Its area is 1,098 square feet.

Higashi Residence

Plates 31–36
Figure 19

■ This garden is an example of a style in which the islets of an inland sea are portrayed. It serves as the front yard for the teahouse and is built along the path between it and the main house. The scenery can be enjoyed from the stone pavement *(nobedan)* and steppingstone path. The shores of the islets are composed of earth mounds covered with moss, and mountain peaks are represented by vertical rocks. White sand depicts the sea on which raked lines abstractly represent a pattern of waves. The garden was designed in 1955 by Mirei Shigemori for Tamiko Higashi, in Takahashi, Okayama Prefecture. It has an area of 1,958 square feet.

FIG. 18. Garden plan. All the plants are beautifully trimmed evergreen shrubs and trees. The one behind the karataki is a camellia. (Daisen-in, Daitoku-ji, Kyoto)

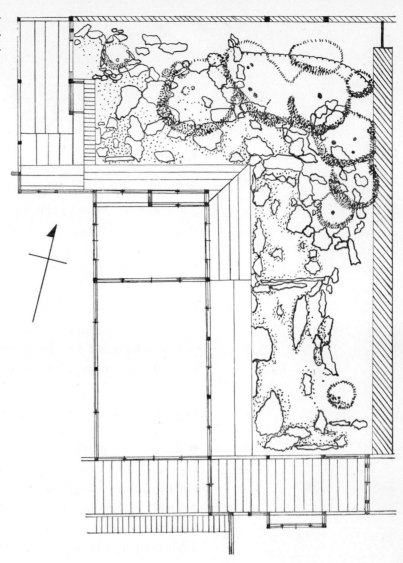

FIG. 19. Garden plan. (Higashi residence, Takahashi, Okayama Pref.)

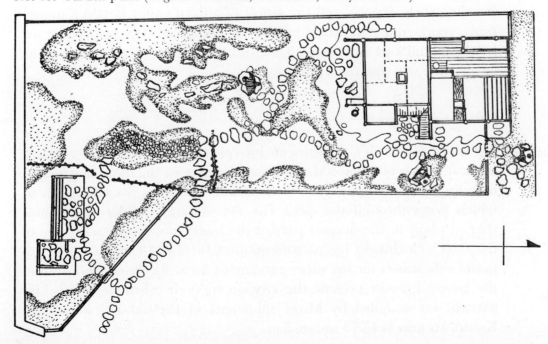

Kanji-in

Plates 37–41
Figure 20
■ While the preceding garden was constructed with mossy earthen piles and rockwork, this one uses only rocks and stones to re-create in miniature the scenery of an inland sea. This garden is not for visual appreciation only, for one can walk within its grounds on the path to the teahouse as in the Higashi residence garden. This, however, has a somewhat more classical quality than does the former garden. Groups of gigantic rocks compose the majestic rockwork, expressing a great degree of movement. One of the largest classical Japanese gardens, it was constructed by the feudal lord Kiyomasa Kato in Kyoto in the early 17th century. The garden's area is 5,380 square feet.

Shinnyo-in

Plates 42–46
Figure 21
■ This stone garden, which lay in ruins for many years, was recently repaired and restored to its former beauty. The scenery with its different shades of green is magnificent and may be compared to the colorful *yamato-e,* a 17th-century style of painting quite independent of Chinese influence. The garden is in Kyoto and dates from the early 17th century. Its area is 1,248 square feet.

Gansen-ji

Plates 47–49
■ This garden was also designed for appreciation while strolling. It is filled with natural beauty, with its upright stone groupings and stream. Bristling rocks express well the aspect of a deep valley between mountains, representing the steep scenery in miniature. It was constructed by the feudal lord Masamune Daté in Osaka in the 17th century. The garden is 1,076 square feet in area.

Fukuda Residence

Plates 50–53
■ This lovely garden presents an interesting panorama depicting the natural setting of Kyoto. Mossy hillocks represent the mountains, commanding a magnificent view. White sand symbolizes the Kamo River, which flows through the city. The dry waterfall under the round-shaped plant in the deepest part of the background represents one of the river's catchment basins, and another *karataki* rockwork at the opposite side stands for the other catchment area. Rocks on and around the mossy hillocks present the city's scenery in abstract form. This garden was designed by Mirei Shigemori in 1960 and is located in Kyoto. Its area is 1,775 square feet.

FIG. 20. Kanji-in garden. (Kanji-in, Kyoto)

FIG. 21. Shinnyo-in garden. (Shinnyo-in, Kyoto)

Daitoku-ji

Plates 54–58
Figure 22
■ Similar to the Shinnyo-in garden, this has a miniature landscape with a large river. There is a dry waterfall rockwork of three rocks by the planting in the southeast part of the garden; it depicts well the quiet flow of Kyoto's large river. On the eastern side are set sixteen scenic stones. These are divided into six groups to give an abstract expression of a natural landscape. The effect of borrowed scenery (*shakkei*) is employed in this garden, which was constructed in Kyoto in the early 17th century by Ten'yu, a priest of this Zen temple. Its area is 14,203 square feet.

Nanso-ji

Plates 59–62
■ Like other dry landscape gardens, this one presents in miniature the scenic beauty of a valley. The effect of the elaborate composition in which rugged pieces of split stones depict the stream is quite unique and dynamic. The weir stones, prominently placed here and there, have been positioned in accordance with definitely allotted proportions. Like the Shinnyo-in garden, this is a magnificent one. Split stones of various colors (red, blue, gray, etc.) give the stream and garden an impression of gorgeousness which is only slightly subdued. Constructed in the early 17th century by the feudal lord and tea master Oribe Furuta, the garden is located in Sakai, Osaka Prefecture. It is 8,877 square feet in area.

Gango-ji

Plates 63–65
Figure 23
■ This garden is characteristic of the miniaturization of Mt. Rozan. The re-creation of a noted scenic view has been one of the most common garden styles in Japan and is an outstanding characteristic of Japanese landscape architecture. This *shukkei* graphically portrays the famous Chinese mountain somewhat as in a *sumi-e,* but in three-dimensional form. The energy generated by the angularity of line and the roughness of the rockwork, which is almost completely buried, make the rocks look like a real outcrop. The viewer is unable to distinguish the border between nature and man's ingenuity with stone and thus appreciates the true value of this wonderful stone garden. It is in Shimoichi-machi, Nara Prefecture, and dates from the 17th century, but its capable designer is unknown. The garden's area is 2,356 square feet.

FIG. 22. Daitoku-ji garden. This exemplifies the technique of borrowed scenery: the outside mountain on the left is incorporated into the design and is seen through the trees from inside the garden. (Daitoku-ji, Kyoto)

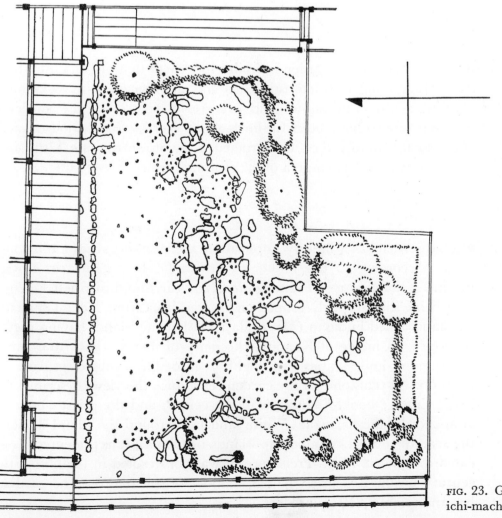

FIG. 23. Garden plan. (Gango-ji, Shimo-ichi-machi, Nara Pref.)

Taizo-in

Plate 66
Figure 24 ▪ This garden shows the highest skill in landscape architecture. The path begins with a cut-stone bridge, passes the large flat stone *(fumi-ishi)* under the planting and then arrives at the cut-stone bridge to the islet. After crossing the second bridge from the islet, the path turns right to the water basin, then across the steppingstones leading to the teahouse. Rocks with the qualities of mountains are used for this garden. Constructed during the 16th century in Kyoto, the garden is said to have been designed by Motonobu Kano, the master painter. It has an area of 4,734 square feet.

Juko-in

Plate 67
Figure 25 ▪ This simple garden was constructed with rockwork in the lichened South Garden. A miniature landscape of Mt. Rozan was built here with a stone bridge between the two islands, one in the east, the other in the west. This garden was designed only for visual appreciation since it has no path. Constructed in Kyoto during the 16th century, the garden's designer is unknown. It has an area of 4,089 square feet.

Hoshun-in

Plate 68 ▪ The scenery of this garden is similar in style to that of Daisen-in, but its distinguishing characteristic is in the simplification of rocks and plantings. Mountain stones and evergreens are used. The garden-maker is said to have been Enshu Kobori, a great Edo period master of landscape architecture. Constructed in Kyoto in the late 17th century, the garden has an area of 9,254 square feet.

Ryotan-ji

Plates 73–77 ▪ This garden has a literary implication and also visualizes a religious event. According to the studies of Edwin O. Reischauer, in Priest Ennin's *The Record of a Pilgrimage to China*, the Buddhist priest Egaku, after being shipwrecked, stopped on his way back from T'ang China at an island called Fudasan (Mt. Fuda). He left the island, having there enshrined an image of Kannon, the deity of mercy. Since that time the island of Fudasan has been highly regarded as a religious shrine of Kannon. All the stones of the garden reproduce the views described in Priest Ennin's book. Fudasan is in the center, and the priest's boat is at anchor by the rockwork. White sand laid around the island depicts the sea. In the background the islands of China are represented. Located in Hikone, Shiga Prefecture, it was constructed in the mid-17th century by the Zen priest Koten, founder of this temple. The garden has an area of 5,810 square feet.

FIG. 24. Taizo-in garden. The path begins with the cut-stone bridge at the upper left. (Taizo-in, Daitoku-ji, Kyoto)

FIG. 25. Juko-in garden. (Juko-in, Kyoto)

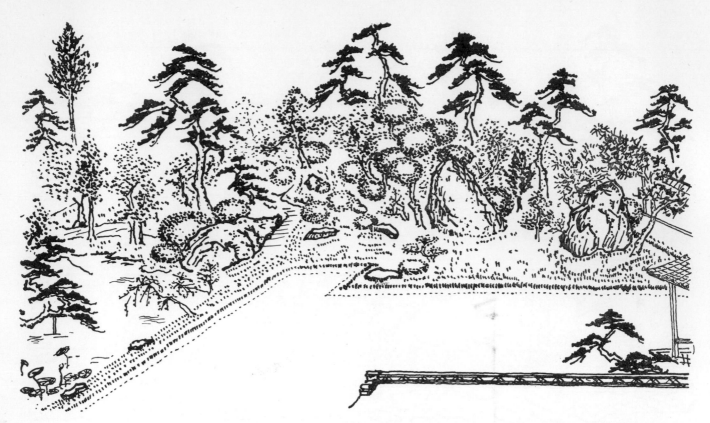

FIG. 26. Shogon-in garden. Two gigantic kei-seki among the trees at the right are called lion rocks because of their shape. This garden was designed for appreciating the huge size and strangeness of these rocks, as well as their material value. (No longer existent)

FIG. 27. Fuji-an garden. The curious mountain-rock kei-seki in the center of the garden was placed to show its monstrous quality. Such stones are displayed for their originality, which renders them rare aesthetic objects, and although this rock simulates a queer bit of mountain scenery it was selected merely as a curiosity piece. (No longer existent)

Gyokudo Art Museum

Plates 78–80 ■ This garden is attached to a museum which was built as a memorial to the Japanese painter Gyokudo Kawai. In it rocks depicting noted distant mountains and other mountain scenery are arranged simply on a white expanse of sand. The size of rock used is moderate to produce a calm atmosphere. The areas west and south of the building are used for the stone garden. In the South Garden only two rocks are placed, and in the southwestern corner a mountain is depicted with rocks. The effect of borrowed scenery is well utilized in this karesansui, as the mountains outside the white earthen wall become part of the design. Thus the simpler the fittings of the garden the more majestic is the view of the background, which seems enclosed and emphasized as in a screen painting. The garden was designed in 1961 by Isoya Yoshida and Ken Nakajima. Located in Tokyo, its area is 3,874 square feet.

Shimane Prefectural Office

Plates 81, 82 ■ In Japan today landscape architecture for public buildings has become quite fashionable. Abstract karesansui blend well with the aesthetics of modern buildings made of reinforced concrete. The courtyard of the Shimane Prefectural Office is one such garden and is constructed entirely of stones and lichened mounds. This novel contemporary garden is designed to be viewed from the windows of the tall building which surrounds it. Using a scattering of *kei-seki,* the coastline of the Sea of Japan is abstractly represented. This design particularly emphasizes the shape of the rocks used, with the result that its beauty is derived much more from these forms than from a resemblance to nature. Designed in 1959 by Kanto Shigemori, who is the son of Mirei Shigemori, the garden is located in Matsue, Shimane Prefecture. Its area is 4,304 square feet.

Tenri Kaikan

Plates 83–85 ■ Built on the roof of a reinforced concrete structure, this garden of a Japanese religious group which teaches Tenri doctrines is partitioned into two parts by split, flat stones. The left side is laid with brown, crushed mountain rocks, and the right with white pebbles. The addition of three rocks of black Swedish granite depicting mountain scenery comprises an abstract garden. Traditionally rocks in Japanese gardens are not artificially handled. This garden, however, is exceptionally well designed with only slight man-made additions to the stones. The ground and polished areas of the rocks are like marble in texture with a black luster, and their sharp edges have a metallic quality. The garden, which gives evidence of the beauty of the sculptor's art, is well worth attention as a unique type of karesansui. Designed by the sculptor Masayuki Nagare in 1961, it is located in Tokyo and has an area of 12,912 square feet.

Tottori Prefectural Office

Plates 86–89 ■ Classical dry landscape gardens were designed principally for visual appreciation. In modern versions, however, a functional aspect has been added to the aesthetic one which the classical gardens have long possessed. In this one, for example, the path of carefully laid stones runs in every direction, which permits more than one viewer at a time to appreciate its arrangement of rocks and plants. Similar to the garden of the Shimane Prefectural Office, this produces a climatic effect in an abstract manner and miniature form. The materials used are mountain rocks. Designed by Kanto Shigemori in 1963, the garden is located in Tottori, Tottori Prefecture. It has an area of 22,596 square feet.

Garden of Kishiwada Castle

Plates 90–94
Figures 28–30 ■ This unusual and modern castle garden was designed with a double purpose: as a landscape in miniature and as the re-creation of the battle formation of Komei Shokatsu (Chuko Kung-ming), the 3rd-century Chinese prime minister, general, and noted strategist. The eight groups of rocks allegorically express his "Battle Formation of the Eight Positions." Focal points of this rockwork are the eight positions of heaven, earth, bird, dragon, cloud, serpent, tiger, and wind, which are arranged

FIG. 28. "Battle Formation of the Eight Positions." (Kishiwada Castle, Osaka)

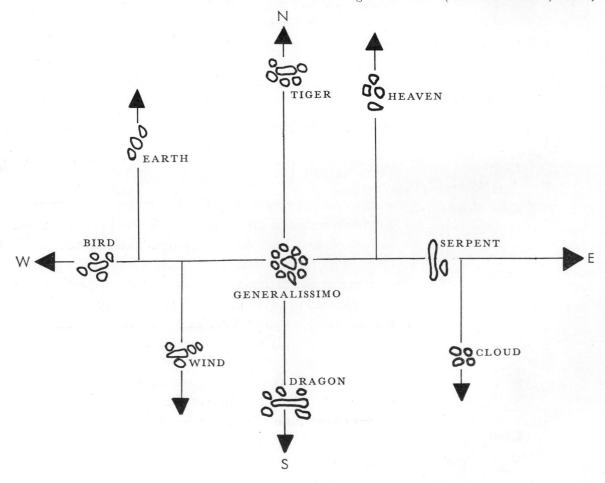

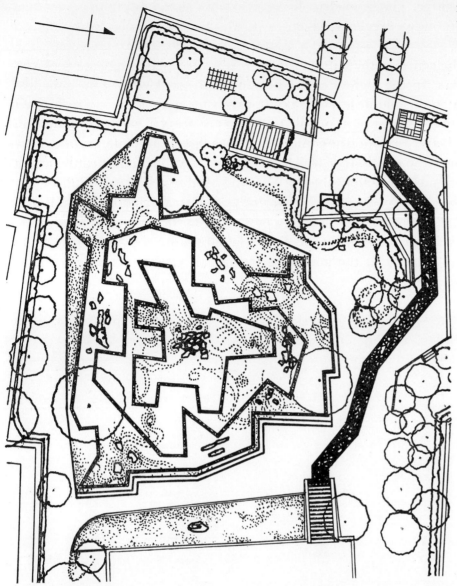

FIG. 29. Garden plan. (Kishiwada Castle, Osaka)

FIG. 30. Detail of garden plan. (Kishiwada Castle, Osaka)

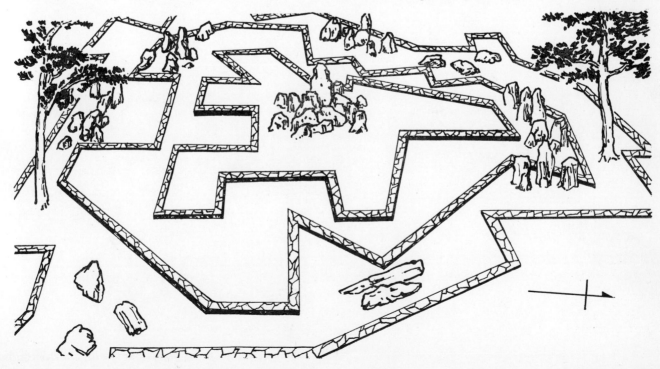

in a circle. The geometric, linear rockwork surrounding these arrangements shows excellent design in its abstract re-creation of the ancient fort.

The center of the battle formation is walled with triplicate rockwork in tiers. In the highest center position is the rockwork of the generalissimo; in the middle level the positions of the tiger and wind are situated; and in the lowest most mobile positions are heaven, earth, bird, dragon, cloud, and serpent. The composition of each unit simulates in an abstract manner the position for which it is named and is simultaneously a classical landscape arrangement. The wavy pattern of white sand depicts a calm sea, exposing the eight varied positions there afloat in an illusory way. This garden is designed to be seen from the windows of the castle, a novel aspect not ordinarily found in karesansui. Designed in 1953 by Mirei Shigemori, the garden is located in Osaka. Its area is 17,754 square feet.

COLOR PLATE 1 *(facing page)*. Sampo-in, Daikaku-ji, Kyoto

PLATE 1. Full view of the rockwork. The rock arrangement looks like part of a natural scene, merging with the surroundings with no appearance of artificiality. Here lies the beauty of karesansui, in which nature and arranged rocks harmoniously blend into one. (Saiho-ji, Kyoto)

PLATE 2.   Upper part of the Saiho-ji kazan rockwork. Looking at the rockwork
one can imagine a stream flowing down over the rocks. (Saiho-ji, Kyoto)

PLATE 3.   Lower part of the rockwork. The rock tiers look as though they
were carved outcrop rocks. Their sharp edges symbolize a steep and soli-
tary valley. (Saiho-ji, Kyoto)

PLATE 4.   Ginkaku-ji kazan rockwork. This rock arrangement is exposed like an outcrop.   Projecting edges of the craggy stones represent peaks of steep mountains. (Ginkaku-ji, Kyoto)

PLATE 5. Full view of the Toko-ji kazan. Although its original appearance is concealed in its present ruinous state, this remains an arrangement worthy of appreciation: the rocks project from the ground like bones from the earth, expressing the dynamic feeling of this rockwork style. (Toko-ji, Kofu, Yamanashi Pref.)

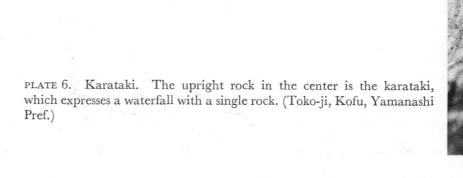

PLATE 6. Karataki. The upright rock in the center is the karataki, which expresses a waterfall with a single rock. (Toko-ji, Kofu, Yamanashi Pref.)

PLATE 7. Full view of the Joei-ji kazan rockwork seen from the veranda off the livingroom. With the center stones in each arrangement as the focus, smaller attendant stones were placed at the sides. Their edge lines are well proportioned as they protrude from the ground to form a triangular composition of good proportions. (Joei-ji, Yamaguchi Pref.)

PLATE 8. View of the rockwork from above. This reveals the distinctive composition of the rock arrangement in the forms of the mountains with their linear beauty. The materials used are mountain rocks either brought by ship from China or carefully selected from every mountainous region of Japan. (Joei-ji, Yamaguchi Pref.)

PLATE 9. Detail of the rockwork. Every miniature mountain is impeccably composed, and each stone seems animated. (Joei-ji, Yamaguchi Pref.)

49

PLATE 10 *(facing page).* Abstract kazan rockwork of the former Yasuda residence garden. The gigantic eroded rock resembles a contemporary abstract sculpture. This magnificent rock stands heroically just over 6½ feet in height and 23 feet in circumference. In the morning, afternoon, and evening changing light and shade alter the stone's appearance. The piercing edges become distinct lines, which form a unique sculptural pattern. This stone attests to the excellence of the Japanese eye, for its abstract sculpturelike form was appreciated in this garden as early as the 17th century. Such natural stones are like living creatures, bewitching viewers with their eternal beauty. (Tokyo)

PLATE 11. Rockwork of Ritsurin Park. A collection of monsterlike stones form this unusual 17th-century kazan. The stones have been handled as objects in the Chinese manner, just as certain nobles in China made this type of arrangement with stones of queer or monstrous shapes. These curious and variegated rocks were found in mountains, valleys, rivers, and the sea. (Ritsurin Park, Takamatsu, Kagawa Pref.)

PLATE 12.   Ogawa residence rockwork. Steppingstones lead from the gate into the garden and to the stone bridge, thus presenting a variety of views. (Ogawa residence, Masuda, Shimane Pref.)

PLATE 14 *(facing page, below)*.   Detail of the rear of the garden. The intensely undulating lines of the upright rocks express well the rough quality and steepness of mountain ranges. (Ogawa residence, Masuda, Shimane Pref.)

PLATE 13. Bird's-eye view of the rear part of the kazan rockwork. The three stones which stand on the white sand beside the bridge symbolize islets. They convey the same sense of pleasure to the viewer as does the boat stone (Plate 15). (Ogawa residence, Masuda, Shimane Pref.)

PLATE 15.   Central view of the garden. All the materials were brought from the seashore and are of a turquoise blue. The rock by the steppingstone path is a boat stone (funa-ishi). (Ogawa residence, Masuda, Shimane Pref.)

PLATE 16 *(facing page, above)*.   Stone bridge and steppingstone path on mossy earth heaps. The teahouse is seen beyond the bamboo fence. A crooked path gives the viewer an opportunity to look at the garden from all directions. (Ogawa residence, Masuda, Shimane Pref.)

PLATE 17 *(facing page, below)*.   Front view of the kazan rockwork and bridge. The bridge, made of two jointed pieces of stone resembling boards, is very simple looking. The rocks standing at its end (hashizoe-ishi) visually stress the bridge's importance. (Ogawa residence, Masuda, Shimane Pref.)

PLATE 18 *(facing page)*. Karataki rockwork and kei-seki. The rocks used in this arrangement have surfaces grooved vertically by nature. Alternating light and shadow present a fantasy of water falling on the stones. Lighting effects were well utilized in this arrangement. (Daisen-in, Daitoku-ji, Kyoto)

PLATE 19. Details of karataki rockwork. The gigantic erect rock in the center rear is the waterfall stone (karataki-ishi). When light strikes its uneven surface, the bright white stone gives the impression of falling water. Attendant rocks (wakiji-ishi) are on either side, and these three comprise the karataki. The flat stone at the foot of the waterfall is a bridge. Rocks arranged near it in the river form a weir and give variety to the stream of white sand. (Daisen-in, Daitoku-ji, Kyoto)

PLATE 20. Karataki rockwork viewed at a distance from the north. The masterful composition of this arrangement maintains its angular and linear shapes regardless of the direction from which it is seen. This interpretation demonstrates a high degree of skill and technique. (Daisen-in, Daitoku-ji, Kyoto)

57

PLATE 21. Detail of upper streams. A small karataki rock arrangement of erect stones is seen in the stream at the upper right. The roughness of uneven surfaces and the steepness of these rocks accurately suggest a many-sectioned valley. The stream flows to lower levels under the bridge in the left foreground. (Daisen-in, Daitoku-ji, Kyoto)

PLATE 22. Turtle-island rockwork. This arrangement is in the northern part of the garden. The turtle island belongs to the idealized world of Taoist demigods and is the arrangement symbolizing prayers for eternal youth and life. To arrange such an island in a garden expresses the owner's hopes for the happiness and prosperity of his family. This part of the garden, therefore, is not in the shukkei style but belongs to a style which describes the Taoist world. (Daisen-in, Daitoku-ji, Kyoto)

PLATE 23. Water basin. This simple arrangement of a stone basin on another stone is in the northern part of the garden. At the left black stones are laid at the place where one washes. Large stones among them serve as steppingstones. The tall erect stone is part of the design and emphasizes the arrangement. (Daisen-in, Daitoku-ji, Kyoto)

PLATE 24. Detail of upper stream and stone-bridge rockwork. The three-tiered white sand stream and the arranged stones effectively suggest a rapid but gentle flow. Attendant rocks on either side of the bridge contribute to the composition. The variously shaped stones that resemble enormous canyon rocks well depict valley scenery and exemplify the good selection of rocks so important in karesansui. (Daisen-in, Daitoku-ji, Kyoto)

PLATE 25. Detail of lower stream. The water flowing rapidly under the bridge runs up against the weir, which gently eases its pace. Scattered scenic stones brought from riverbeds are almost buried to resemble an outcrop and suggest the stream's depth. Their surfaces are well worn and have a hard quality. (Daisen-in, Daitoku-ji, Kyoto)

PLATE 27. Detail of incense stone viewed from above. This stone not only functions as the stand on which incense is burned but is also a kei-seki expressing the depth and clearness of a rough stream in a valley. The stone is moderate in dimension, maintaining fine balance of composition, and thus represents the essence of landscape gardening. (Daisen-in, Daitoku-ji, Kyoto)

PLATE 26. Kei-seki. This hard mountain stone with a fine-grained surface resembling wood is called jinko-seki, meaning incense stone. When visitors come the host burns incense on this stone to make the air fragrant. This shows his courteousness to the guests. (Daisen-in, Daitoku-ji, Kyoto)

PLATE 28.   Detail of the lower stream and boat rock. The white sand stream is transformed into a vast but gentle river. This is a perfectly composed scene including the floating fishing boat and the distant mountains against the field. (Daisen-in, Daitoku-ji, Kyoto)

PLATE 29.   Detail of garden background. The triangular stone in the back symbolizes the magnificent form of a noted mountain viewed from a distance. Moss used at the foot of the mountain expresses its gentle contours. (Daisen-in, Daitoku-ji, Kyoto)

PLATE 30.   Detail of boat rock. A fishing boat is represented on the large river. The bow shows movement toward the right, and the boat appears to be floating on the river. (Daisen-in, Daitoku-ji, Kyoto)

PLATE 31. Nobedan and central part of the Higashi residence garden. The stone pavement surrounded with moss is a nobedan. Guests invited to the tea ceremony enter through the gate, walk on the nobedan, and following the steppingstones pass through the bamboo gate. Each step presents a different view which is both visually stimulating and spiritually satisfying. The scenery at the left is a shukkei rockwork. Such a garden encourages the guest to appreciate the deep emotional qualities integrated with its construction. An aura of inner peace surrounds those fortunate enough to wander through such quiet premises embodying the elegant and tasteful beauty of spirit found in this fine Japanese garden. (Higashi residence, Takahashi, Okayama Pref.)

64

PLATE 32. View of the garden. Patterns in the piled soil covered with green moss represent the seashore; the rhythmical expression of the energetic curves gives a cheerful impression. The stone materials were quarried from a river in the neighboring mountain district. They are small in size but beautifully shaped, and their sharp edges have a distinct, vivid quality. (Higashi residence, Takahashi, Okayama Pref.)

PLATE 33. Central part of the garden. The stone water basin is a tsukubai. Following the steppingstones the guest is brought to a halt before it, where he washes his hands and rinses his mouth before proceeding to the teahouse. The upright stone in the upper right corner is the main peak which emphasizes the angular lines of the other arranged stones. The composition of the rock arrangements has a definite rhythm, the well-balanced placement of the stones' edges showing strong movement toward the main peak. Mossy banks describe beautiful curves supporting the lines of the arranged stones. One cannot help but appreciate the skill of this construction. (Higashi residence, Takahashi, Okayama Pref.)

PLATE 34. View from the stepping-stones. When seen from the steppingstones the garden looks dynamic and presents a magnificent view. The islet with moss provides an attractive accent. Each arrangement of three stones forms a triangle, with the center stone as its apex. (Higashi residence, Takahashi, Okayama Pref.)

PLATE 35. Detail of the garden peninsula. Looking from the nobedan one finds a small projecting peninsula of moss on the white sand. The composition of the rock arrangement blends well with it, as the colors of the sand, moss, and stones add to the quiet, tasteful (shibui) tone of the whole garden, creating an impression not easily forgotten. (Higashi residence, Takahashi, Okayama Pref.)

PLATE 36. Nobedan. Pavement of this type is composed of small stones and hardened clay earth. The striking aesthetic effect is achieved by surrounding the nobedan with moss; this keeps it in harmony with the garden's scenery. The combination of practical and aesthetic elements is adroitly managed in this garden. (Higashi residence, Takahashi, Okayama Pref.)

PLATE 37. Central part of the Kanji-in garden. This garden, though unkept now, still bears traces of its former magnificence. The huge rocks on the left have been arranged into a kazan, a construction requiring the highest technique and skill because the rocks are placed without any soil or sand between them. This is the most difficult stone-garden construction. (Kanji-in, Kyoto)

PLATE 38. Front part of the garden. Huge attendant stones have been arranged on both sides of the steps to conceal them and to function as scenic rocks. Such rocks which have a decorative as well as practical purpose are called yaku-ishi. All the stones in the arrangement are from rivers and mountains. (Kanji-in, Kyoto)

PLATE 39.   Gigantic dry waterfall rockwork and stream. The dynamic gravity and figurative beauty of the rocks describe this shukkei's resemblance to sumi-e. An air of severity is expressed by this typical stone garden, in which no plants are used. (Kanji-in, Kyoto)

PLATE 40. Detail of the rear part of the garden. The path which leads from the entrance (Plate 38) eventually arrives at the island and continues over the stone bridge on the left. By following this path guests enjoy the varied scenery on their way to the teahouse. (Kanji-in, Kyoto)

PLATE 41. Detail of the central rockwork. The group of rocks at the upper stream of gravel is the karataki arrangement. The stream flows down under the natural stone bridge and meets the weir. Water then falls down the cliff, at the foot of which is a triangular water-dividing stone (mizuwake-ishi) which separates the flow into two parts. (Kanji-in, Kyoto)

PLATE 42. Full view of the Shinnyo-in garden. The rippling stream, composed of black and blue stones, is entirely surrounded by mossy hillocks and rock mountains. Although built on a small scale, this garden has such refinement that it refreshes the spirit with its calm atmosphere. (Shinnyo-in, Kyoto)

PLATE 43. Detail of the stream. Small stones depict the ripples of the stream in a realistic manner. (Shinnyo-in, Kyoto)

PLATE 44. Full view from the lower stream. Running from the dry waterfall in back of the cut-stone bridge (Plate 43), the stream snakes down around the mossy land. All the rocks arranged around it are kei-seki. (Shinnyo-in, Kyoto)

PLATE 45. Detail of the lower stream. The rock arrangement of kei-seki on both curving points give variety to the scene. (Shinnyo-in, Kyoto)

PLATE 46. Detail of rock composition. Ripples of black and blue stones ruffle the stream, giving a rich quality to the garden. This stream expresses the fine individuality of its construction which is different from the usual sand, gravel, and pebbles. Essential in making a karesansui is the offering of such creative beauty as this, which is in harmony with the surroundings as a whole. This originality lifts dry landscaping design into the realm of art. (Shinnyo-in, Kyoto)

PLATE 47.   Central part of the Gansen-ji garden. The four rocks stand confronting one another and depict a mountain scene with sharpness and energy. White sand at the right represents a calm stream, and the round flat stones at the left express the current of a rapidly flowing stream. The two meet in the center. (Gansen-ji, Osaka)

74

PLATE 48. Front part of the garden. (Gansen-ji, Osaka)

PLATE 49. Rear part of the garden. The stream, having flowed more strongly, turns again into calm, white sand and moves under the stone bridge (*upper left*) into a field. On both banks flat kei-seki and roundly trimmed plants depict a scene of mountains and fields in miniature. (Gansen-ji, Osaka)

PLATE 50. Southern part of the Fukuda residence garden. Arranged scenic rocks accentuate the mossy hillocks, which give the garden a unique beauty. (Fukuda residence, Kyoto)

PLATE 51. Full view of the garden. Mountain ranges wind through almost two-thirds of the southern part, vividly delineating the garden. (Fukuda residence, Kyoto)

PLATE 52. Aerial view of the southeastern part of the garden. The garden includes a stone bridge and stepping-stones. At the right a group of four rocks forms a dry waterfall. Three rocks at the upper left form another karataki. Together these two symbolize the water sources of Kyoto. (Fukuda residence, Kyoto)

PLATE 53. Central part of the garden. The stones set in pavement represent the curved shore of the river and were selected for their river or marine qualities. (Fukuda residence, Kyoto)

PLATE 54. Southern part of the Daitoku-ji garden. The sand patterns depict rippling water. In midstream are placed two flat black stones functioning as kei-seki. With moss encircling them, these become an island unit. The background of white sand, scenic stones, and trimmed plantings forms a landscape in abstract form—a fantastic spectacle of great force. (Daitoku-ji, Kyoto)

PLATE 55. Detail of the island seen from the veranda. (Daitoku-ji, Kyoto)

PLATE 56. Eastern part of the garden. Each of the six groups of sixteen stones forms a unique landscape and presents a different scene for the enjoyment of viewers. (Daitoku-ji, Kyoto)

PLATE 57. Detail of the eastern part of the garden. A magnificent scene is presented by five rocks, one upright, and four with horizontal interest. River stones of a bluish hue are used here. The standing stone with white vertical stripes is a karataki. (Daitoku-ji, Kyoto)

PLATE 58. Sand patterns in the southern part of the garden. Straight and wavy patterns are raked parallel by turns. Both lines symbolize the gentle flow of the majestic river. Rough granite chips compose the sand. (Daitoku-ji, Kyoto)

PLATE 59. View of the upper and central parts of the Nanso-ji garden. The stream of vari-colored split stones vividly contrasts with and enlivens the weir stones. (Nanso-ji, Osaka)

PLATE 60. Upper garden seen from the midpoint. The stream flows slowly, turning to the right. Scattered kei-seki provide a scenic complement to the flow, thus adding to the effect of the garden. (Nanso-ji, Osaka)

PLATE 61. Full-length view of the garden and stream. The flow becomes wider in the lower stream where stepping-stones continue the path, placed as they are in the Gan-sen-ji garden. (Nanso-ji, Osaka)

81

PLATE 62.   Upper part of the garden. The group of standing rocks behind the stone
bridge forms a karataki arrangement, which looks as though water were really rushing
over it. Weir stones placed below the bridge give variety to the stream's movement.
(Nansə-ji, Osaka)

82

PLATE 63. Central Gango-ji rockwork viewed from east to north. A water basin is seen at the lower right. Clean water stands in the carved depression. (Gango-ji, Shimoichi-machi, Nara Pref.)

PLATE 64. Central rockwork viewed from north to east. The arranged rocks, resembling an outcrop with their angular edges confronting one another, depict a steep and severe landscape. (Gango-ji, Shimoichi-machi, Nara Pref.)

PLATE 65. Central view of the garden. The design of this karesansui is such that it should not be viewed from the veranda but instead from the garden path. One descends from the veranda to the steppingstones and crosses the bridge, then goes up the stone steps to reach the other building in the distance. This design is typical of a garden which serves both practical and aesthetic purposes. (Gango-ji, Shimoichi-machi, Nara Pref.)

PLATE 66. Central view of the Taizo-in garden. This idealized landscape in miniature presents islands and the sea. The arrangement, emphasizing the angular forms of the stones, has a majestic expression. The design's pictorial effect is reminiscent of sumi-e. (Taizo-in, Daitoku-ji, Kyoto)

PLATE 67.   Central view of the Juko-in garden. Green moss symbolizes a vast lake. The erect rocks at left are very characteristic of the landscape they represent and give the effect of a sumi-e of Mt. Rozan. Focusing on the stone bridge, the scene makes a light and elegant garden arrangement. (Juko-in, Kyoto)

PLATE 68. Central part of the rockwork of the Hoshun-in garden. Large trimmed plants portray the scenery of a deep mountain valley, and the erect rocks nearby represent waterfalls. A white stone in front of the falls forms a boat. (Hoshun-in, Kyoto)

PLATE 69.   Tiger rock (tora-ishi). This rock has a tiger-skin pattern of wavy brown and reddish stripes. The product of a river the rock is of a fine, hard quality. It is valued at $9,000.

PLATE 70.   Thread-strung rock (itokake-ishi). This is a product of the upper part of a valley. White hairlines twist the gray surface like threads. It is also valued at $9,000.

PLATE 71. Angular armor rock (yoroi-ishi). The texture of this rock, resembling the tucks in a suit of Japanese armor, gave this mei-seki its name. It is valued at $10,000.

PLATE 72. Rounded armor rock. This rock is the same type as that in Plate 71 but shows fewer tucks. Its value is $5,000.

PLATES 73 and 74. Full views of the Fudasan rockwork at Ryotan-ji. The huge upright rock projecting at the center is the rock of the deity of mercy (Kannon-seki) that symbolizes the image of Kannon, or the Bodhisattva. The garden uses mountain rocks of fine quality. (Ryotan-ji, Hikone, Shiga Pref.)

PLATE 75. Fudasan rockwork viewed from the veranda. (Ryotan-ji, Hikone, Shiga Pref.)

PLATE 76. Detail of the boat stone. The boat in which Priest Egaku sailed is symbolized by this naturally shaped stone. (Ryotan-ji, Hikone, Shiga Pref.)

PLATE 77. Fudasan rockwork viewed from the front. This masterful composition with its sharp edges and lines is impeccably arranged. Well suited to a Zen temple, it has stability, majesty, and dignity. Crushed mountain rock is used for the sea of sand. (Ryotan-ji, Hikone, Shiga Pref.)

PLATE 78.   Full-length view of the South Garden of the Gyokudo Art Museum to the west. The black rock in the foreground is a kei-seki. The outer edge of the triangular rock extends toward it. These rocks are extremely well proportioned and balanced. (Gyokudo Art Museum, Tokyo)

PLATE 79.   Full view of the South Garden from the veranda. The enzan-seki still maintains its triangular form and fine proportional relationship to the scenic rock, even while viewed from the north. This fact attests to the skill of the garden's composition. (Gyokudo Art Museum, Tokyo)

PLATE 80 *(facing page)*. South Garden and its borrowed scenery. The triangular stone in the center front is mountainous in quality and simulates Mt. Fuji. (Gyokudo Art Museum, Tokyo)

PLATE 81. Bird's-eye view of the Shimane Prefectural Office. The material used is river rock from this district. (Shimane Prefectural Office, Matsue, Shimane Pref.)

PLATE 82. Full-length view of the center of the garden. The starfish patterns of the moss mounds abstractly re-create the coastline and islands of the Sea of Japan. Sand patterns called jokai-ha (literally blue sea waves) symbolize a calm expanse of sea. (Shimane Prefectural Office, Matsue, Shimane Pref.)

PLATE 83.   Central view of the roof garden at Tenri Kaikan. The surfaces of the kei-seki are ground and polished as smooth as glass in order to reflect sunshine or the dim light of a cloudy day or evening. (Tenri Kaikan, Tokyo)

PLATE 84. Full view of the roof garden. None of the naturalism usually seen in classical gardens is found here. The garden possesses only the beauty of stones existing as objects of fine shape and form. (Tenri Kaikan, Tokyo)

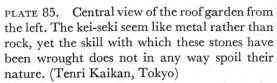

PLATE 85. Central view of the roof garden from the left. The kei-seki seem like metal rather than rock, yet the skill with which these stones have been wrought does not in any way spoil their nature. (Tenri Kaikan, Tokyo)

PLATE 86. Rockwork of the Tottori Prefectural Office garden. All the kei-seki project upward, giving a rough and dynamic expression. Each line of the rock arrangement is concentrated and balanced, and the lichened mound at the center shows a rhythmic proportion throughout. The path is of mortared slate. (Tottori Prefectural Office, Tottori Pref.)

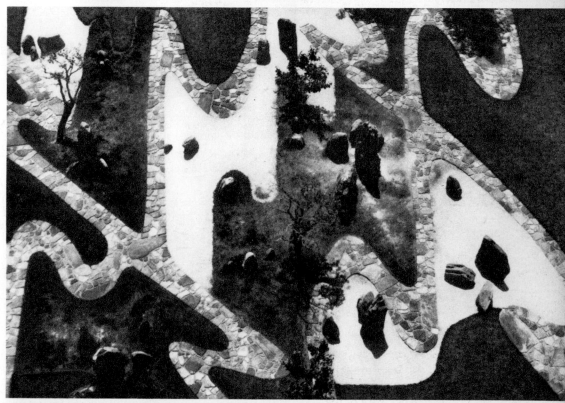

PLATE 87. A bird's-eye view of the garden. The garden path is designed to lead the viewer in any of six directions to appreciate all the rocks and plantings. (Tottori Prefectural Office, Tottori Pref.)

PLATE 88. A bird's-eye view of the central part of the garden. The garden has a splendid allotment of space. (Tottori Prefectural Office, Tottori Pref.)

PLATE 89. Central rockwork. The balance and proportion of the composition attract the eye, as the designer intended. (Tottori Prefectural Office, Tottori Pref.)

PLATE 90. Rockwork of the Kishiwada Castle garden viewed from west to east. The arrangement of rocks in the foreground represents the symbolic position of the bird. (Kishiwada Castle, Osaka)

PLATE 91 *(facing page, above)*. Bird's-eye view of the garden. The focal point of the design is the rockwork of the generalissimo at the center. The geometric patterns copy the design of the ancient fort and depict the rock walls in a manner similar to a relief, each wall being 8 inches high. The garden is designed in three tiers. (Kishiwada Castle, Osaka)

PLATE 92 *(facing page, below)*. Generalissimo rockwork viewed from the southwest. The position of wind can be seen in the right foreground. (Kishiwada Castle, Osaka)

first is the Shumisen, expressing the Buddhist view of the universe in which the sun, moon, and planets rotate around Mt. Shumisen, the holy place of Buddha. (*Kuzan-hakkai,* another term for Shumisen, refers to the nine mountains and eight seas depicting the world where Buddha is enthroned.) The second is the rockwork of the sacred precinct where a Buddhist image is installed, and the third is the rockwork which symbolizes a stage of Zen enlightenment. These three express the essence of Zen, and the gardens seem to speak to the viewer of their spiritual and mystic content. The outstanding aesthetics of Japanese stone gardens are nowhere more evident than in the karesansui of Zen temples. These gardens are interesting to the viewer not only for the beauty of their stone placement but also because they incorporate symbolism with religious implications. This endows them with creative and articulate qualities transcending appearance; and people believed in the stone and plant images of Buddha, making fetishes of them.

Ryoan-ji

Plates 95–98
Figures 31, 32
■ The Shumisen rockwork of the Ryoan-ji garden symbolizes the Buddhist world where an invisible figure of Buddha is believed to exist and is worshiped. This garden is simultaneously a mystic place and an appropriately grand setting for the stone deities. It was constructed in the early 17th century in Kyoto. The garden's area is 3,228 square feet.

Shoden-ji

Plates 99, 100
■ While the Ryoan-ji garden depicts the world of Shumisen with rockwork and sand, the garden of Shoden-ji symbolizes it with sand and azalea plants. A group of seven azaleas at the right forms Mt. Shumisen; a group of five smaller plants in the middle and another of three at the left end depict the eight mountains of a *kuzan-hakkai*. In May, the season for azaleas, these plants have blossoms of pure red, turning the garden into a small world of color. In late autumn the surrounding forests become a gold-tinged landscape which envelops the garden. Designed and built in Kyoto in the middle of the 17th century, it has an area of 1,569 square feet.

FIG. 31. Shumisen rockwork. (Ryoan-ji, Kyoto)

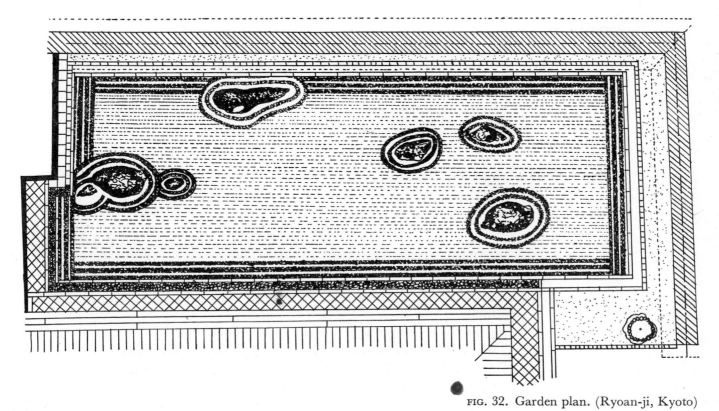

FIG. 32. Garden plan. (Ryoan-ji, Kyoto)

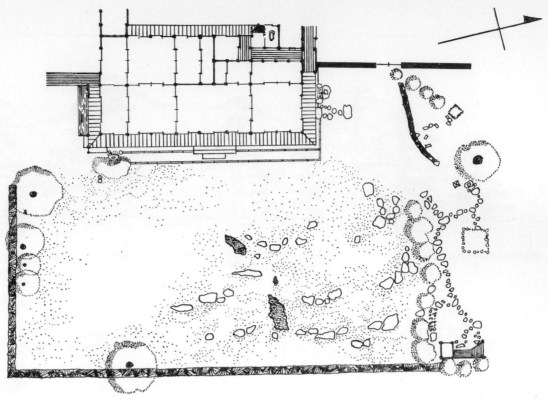

FIG. 33. Garden plan. (Entsu-ji, Kyoto)

Entsu-ji

Plate 101
Figure 33

■ The rockwork shows clearly that this karesansui symbolizes the Buddhist world view. It includes a fine combination of more than forty rocks and a natural outcrop. Compared with the concrete illustrations of *kuzan-hakkai* in the Ryoan-ji and the Shoden-ji gardens, this landscape is quite abstract. Its green moss represents the eight seas, and the mountain in the background at the farthest point is Mt. Hiei. Thus the scenery of the holy mountain is borrowed, as in the Shoden-ji garden, to symbolize the image of Buddha. The beauty felt when viewing this garden is profound and mysterious. Built in Kyoto in the middle of the 18th century, the garden has an area of 2,092 square feet.

Saiho-ji

Plates 102, 103

■ In Kyoto the Saiho-ji garden is known as the "Moss Temple." Part of it is widely acknowledged as the best example of a karesansui in the Shumisen style. The composition of the rockwork represents *kuzan-hakkai* in an abstract, concentrated form, and the majestic Shumisen rock emits a perfect structural beauty appropriate to the holy place of Buddha.

Formerly this temple was a seminary for the Zen Buddhist priesthood. Many a seeker of truth sat on the meditation rock (Plate 103) facing Mt. Shumisen while meditating and seeking the essence of Buddhism. Thus this rockwork was not constructed for appreciation but as a mysterious and sacred place of meditation. The rocks of the Moss Temple have the most definite Zen quality of all the Japanese gardens considered. This garden was designed by the Zen priest Muso Kokushi in the middle of the 14th century and is located in Kyoto. Its area is 4,184 square feet.

Komyo Zen-in

Plates 104–107
Figure 34

■ The garden's triplet rockwork representing three Buddhist images is called *sanzon-seki*. These three images are very often the subject of Japanese religious painting and are here embodied in three-dimensional form. This garden depicts the world of a Buddhist tale, stressing the three images. Although the triplet rockwork may also be considered as a *karataki* (which is a variation of the *sanzon-seki* style) this garden is primarily iconographic.

The arranged azalea plants in the rear of the white sand pond describe patterns of serene waters *(jokai-ha)*. These symbolize the state of mind of one enlightened by Zen. The *sanzon-seki* stand in the middle of the garden among the serene waters. Scattered rocks, like radiant rays here and there in all parts of the garden, represent halos of the holy images. The pond of white sand is not a naturalistic but a symbolic depiction: "Clouds do not arise over the mountain peaks; they fall to the bottom of ponds." This statement compares the clean state of an enlightened mind to clouds reflected on the water's surface. Thus the pond expresses a holy stage of Zen enlightenment, and the garden's profound beauty is internally felt. Designed in 1938 by Mirei Shigemori, the garden is located in Kyoto. Its area is 17,259 square feet.

FIG. 34. Garden plan. (Komyo Zen-in, Tofuku-ji, Kyoto)

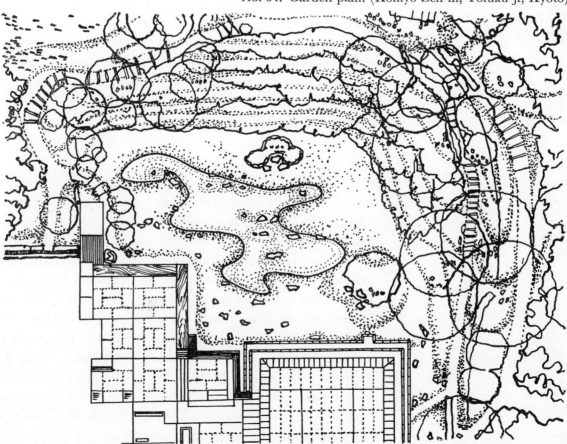

Daichi-ji

Plates 108–110 ■ The design of this garden's planting is rather baroque by contrast to other Zen gardens. Seven images of Buddha are placed among the large, wave-patterned azalea plants. These images symbolize the extension of the Buddha's wisdom through past, present, and future. They are expressed here with seven small plants arranged in a neat and compact manner. Patterns of serene waters symbolic of Zen enlightenment are those of a selfless world. With these images the garden expresses a profound and self-effacing world. This garden was built in Minakuchimachi, Shiga Prefecture, in the early 17th century. It has an area of 1,674 square feet.

Jizo-in

Plates 111–115 ■ This garden contains sixteen images of Rakan (Arhat in Sanskrit), depicted with stones. Rakan, one of Buddha's advanced disciples, is a human figure, yet he changes into an image of Buddha. Thus he inhabits the boundary area between this world and Nirvana, serving as a mediator for human beings as they enter the next world. The scattered stones among the evergreen grove are images of Rakan and make the garden into the sacred precinct of a religious painting. The stones used here are regarded as holy images of the metamorphosed Rakan. This garden can be viewed as an elaborate illustration of Buddhist iconography. Each stone has an independent existence, and the entire composition keeps the rocky landscape in a strange state of balance. The garden was designed by the Zen priest Korei in the early 18th century. Located in Kyoto, it has an area of 3,138 square feet.

Tokai-an

Plates 116–118 ■ This garden is in a courtyard surrounded by temple buildings. Only seven stones are arranged on the expanse of white sand. The composition, made by placing a small rock between two triplet-rock formations *(sanzon-seki),* has interesting proportional and rhythmical effects. It symbolizes the Solar Buddha (Nichimen Butsu) and the Lunar Buddha (Gechimen Butsu). According to a scriptural reference, the former lives only a day while the latter lives for 1,800 years. This courtyard has become a sacred place, with its arrangement of the temporal and everlasting Buddha images. The stone placed between the two rock groups is called *haku-un-seki* and symbolizes a white cloud. This garden thus represents images of Buddha in a bank of clouds. It is a significant karesansui, one which is very appropriate to a Zen temple. The garden was designed and built in Kyoto in 1814 by the Zen priest Toboku and has an area of 262 square feet.

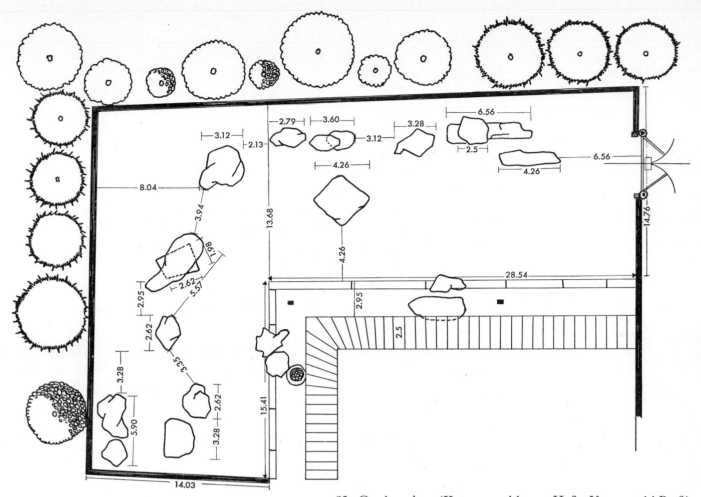

FIG. 35. Garden plan. (Katsura residence, Hofu, Yamaguchi Pref.)

Katsura Residence

Plates 119–124
Figure 35 ■ Although constructed well over two centuries ago, this karesansui looks very modern. Particularly unique and beautiful is the L-shaped rockwork. The garden portrays the state of Zen enlightenment described in an ancient Chinese Buddhist tale in which a hare and an oyster (*bo* in Chinese) conceive on a night of the full moon by absorbing moonlight into their bodies. This allegory suggests that human intelligence should be as pure and innocent as these pregnancies by the spirit of the moon. It is the state of mind produced by Buddha's teaching and the spiritual awakening it brings that are of this purity. Without knowing these implications one cannot understand or appreciate the aesthetics of this karesansui. Such inner depth of interpretation is fundamental to Japanese art, particularly in the case of the Zen garden.

The L-shaped rockwork representing the hare and the round rock representing the oyster are the most important of the composition. A Buddhist landscape centering on the hare rockwork is built in the East Garden, and a landscape of the world of the Taoist demigod-hermits is found in the adjacent South Garden. Both gardens have independent landscapes. On the border between them the rockworks of the hare and the oyster are arranged. A complete view of the rockwork may be enjoyed in whichever garden one stands. This garden masterpiece was designed by Umpei Tadaharu Katsura in 1713 and is located in Hofu, Yamaguchi Prefecture. It has an area of 847 square feet.

Ryogen-in

Plates 125, 126   ■ The East Garden of this karesansui depicts a scene in which a drop of water has fallen into a vast sea. According to a Zen teaching, "Buddhism is something like the sea. When a drop of rain falls there, a large ripple is described on the sea. A human being, by throwing himself into the sea [Buddha's world] also causes a great ripple." The conception of this karesansui is the depiction of a mind-seeking enlightenment in Zen. It expresses the idea that one who intends to illuminate himself must be willing to throw himself into the sea of Buddha, believing that like the raindrop he will find the Way. This garden was designed by the Zen priest Tokei in the 15th century and is located in Kyoto. It has an area of 105 square feet.

The West Garden also portrays a calm state of Zen. White sand symbolizes the vast ocean, while the green-lichened mounds are mountain ranges in miniature. This symbolic landscape gives the impression of motion in stillness. The West Garden was designed by Nabeshima in 1958 and is 314 square feet in area.

Kozen-ji

Plates 127, 128   ■ Buddhist enlightenment is the realm of the higher self. The sand patterns and rockwork of this karesansui are elements in the symbolic description of this enlightened world. Mountain ranges rising above the clouds metaphorically express the self that is as vast and free as cloud banks. White sand symbolizes clouds, and its patterns well express their appearance. The rockwork is composed in groupings of three, five, and seven, which give an aesthetically pleasing proportional effect. Located near a mountain, this garden gives one a sense of peace and spiritual realization. The garden was designed by Mirei Shigemori in 1963 and is in Fukushima-machi, Nagano Prefecture. Its area is 10,652 square feet.

Ryogin-an

Plates 129–136   ■ This landscape is a scenic description of the Zen teaching of the Rinzai sect. Rinzai (Lin-chi), who was one of the greatest Chinese Zen priests of the 7th century, has been described as being "as majestic as the movement of a tiger, as the running of a dragon, as the striking of thunder and lightning, and as the turning of the earth." On the west side of the temple a dragon is depicted appearing among black clouds. The patterns of the clouds, depicted with black sand, give movement to the garden's composition. The garden was designed by Mirei Shigemori in 1964 and is in Kyoto. It has an area of 3,443 square feet.

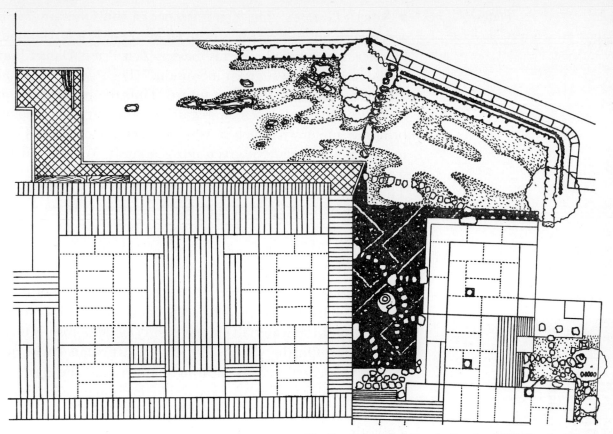

FIG. 36. Garden plan. (South Garden of Zuiho-in, Kyoto)

Zuiho-in

Plates 137–141

Figure 36

■ SOUTH GARDEN. This garden also depicts a state of Zen enlightenment with a Chinese landscape in miniature. The Zen implication is derived from the 26th article, "Hyakujo, Mt. Daiyuho," of the Zen scripture *Hekiganroku* (The Blue Rock Collection). In it a Buddhist disciple asks Ekai Hyakujo (Pao-chang), the famous Chinese priest who established the Zen monastic rules and practices in the 8th century, "Master, is there anything different from other sects in the study and practice of Zen?" The master responds, "Behold me. I am sitting very correctly. Do I not look self-assured? There is nothing at all different from ordinary practices in the study of Zen. Seat yourself as Mt. Hyakujo does." (The priest was referring to Mt. Daiyuho, the site of a magnificent waterfall and the place where he lived.)

The garden expresses this catechism between the master and his disciple. A rockwork symbolizing Mt. Hyakujo is constructed on the lichened mound. On its right a large lake full of water from the falls is depicted with white sand. This description of the majestic landscape of China exalts Priest Hyakujo's practice of Zen. Such a garden, which incorporates a beautiful design expressing a Zen teaching, epitomizes the Zen karesansui. Herein lie the aesthetic quality and creativeness of Japanese garden design, particularly of the stone garden: rockwork of miniature mountains is no longer abstract nature; it is Priest Ekai Hyakujo's majestic figure sitting correctly in meditation, and the stones personify his religious spirit. The garden, designed by Mirei Shigemori in 1961, is in Kyoto. Its area is 5,154 square feet.

Plates 142–144 ■ NORTH GARDEN. The Zen reference of this karesansui is taken from a sentence in the certificate given to Zen Priest Daimon Fuo, the founder of this temple, by his master, Zen Priest Daitsu Buchi: "Sleep confidently against a green mountain." The "green mountain" in this instance symbolizes the great future. Thus the phrase tells one to carry himself with confidence in regard to the future, although what it brings is unknown. Such a view is essential to Zen. The miniature mountains are made of green moss mounds. White sand forms a seascape. All the rocks in the sea were chosen for their scenic qualities. This Kyoto garden covering an area of 3,551 square feet was also designed by Mirei Shigemori in 1961.

Sangen-in

Plates 145–147 ■ This stone garden is a typical *shukkei,* as are many of those discussed in the first chapter. At the left in the background is a *karataki* rockwork. In front of it the waterfall's stone basin *(takitsubo-ishi)* is placed deep in the ground. On the white sand, *kei-seki* articulated with moss are arranged in an aesthetically pleasing manner, and the garden has a composition similar to that of a *sumi-e.* The meaning underlying this *shukkei,* however, was inspired by a state of Zen enlightenment, as were the two Zuiho-in gardens. This karesansui depicts the words of the 16th-century Zen priest Soen Shun'oku: "yesterday's clouds." Interpreting in the Zen manner, the reference to the sky of yesterday indicates a bright clear sky without a trace of clouds. This symbolizes a clear state of mind, which is expressed in this garden by a miniature version of a vast landscape. The garden was designed in 1960 by Kaido Fuji and Seizan Ito and has an area of 3,443 square feet. It is located in Kyoto.

COLOR PLATE 2 *(facing page).* Shoden-ji, Kyoto

PLATE 95. Ryoan-ji garden. The stone of Shumisen is the focal point in the design. Other stones are placed in line with its angular edges and the vital force radiating from it. (Ryoan-ji, Kyoto)

PLATE 96. Detail of the Shumisen rockwork. The small rock in front of the Shumisen rock complements by providing the radiating lines of the design. The majestic figure of the Shumisen rockwork looks appropriately imposing as the holy place of Buddha. (Ryoan-ji, Kyoto)

PLATE 97. Panoramic view of the garden. The rockwork at the extreme left is Mt. Shumisen, and those on the right depict the other eight mountains. White sand symbolizes the eight seas. (Ryoan-ji, Kyoto)

PLATE 98. Three mountain peaks. These are three of the nine mountains which with eight seas depict the Buddhist universe. (Ryoan-ji, Kyoto)

PLATES 99 and 100. Bird's-eye views of the Shoden-ji garden. The fifteen azalea plants seem afloat on the sea of white sand, and the background beyond the garden wall extends to the range of mountains including Mt. Hiei. Harmonious blending with this magnificent landscape brings out the subtlety of the garden and is an excellent example of the borrowed landscape technique, which can be an important factor in the creation of a fine garden. Incorporating the form of Mt. Hiei has spiritual significance in addition to its visual role in the composition, for this mountain is considered to be holy and inviolate as the birthplace of Japanese Zen Buddhism. Thus borrowing this scenery for the garden is like including an image of Buddha himself. It is believed that if the viewer concentrates deeply on the garden the Buddha will appear before him in this world of Shumisen, beyond time and space. (Shoden-ji, Kyoto)

PLATE 101. Central part of the Entsu-ji Shumisen rockwork. The rocks are arranged on a thick moss ground and look entirely natural. This composition demonstrates the skill of the maker, for it gives the least possible indication of artificial handling, and the viewer can appreciate in this rockwork truly excellent technique. (Entsu-ji, Kyoto)

121

PLATE 102.   Saiho-ji Shumisen rockwork. The projecting rock in the center represents Mt. Shumisen, and rocks symbolizing the eight mountains surround the main religious peak. Forceful and dynamic composition expresses well the stern, sacred place. (Saiho-ji, Kyoto)

PLATE 103. Meditation rock. This rock is placed on a small hill overlooking the Shumisen rockwork. (Saiho-ji, Kyoto)

PLATE 104.   Central part of the Komyo Zen-in garden. The holy triplet rocks stand
at the foot of the three round azalea plants in the center rear. (Komyo Zen-in, Tofuku-
ji, Kyoto)

PLATE 105.   Triplet rockwork. Three upright rocks stand at the foot of the plantings
to portray the images of Buddha. In spring, the azaleas behind the rocks bloom in
rosy profusion, while the background turns red in autumn. (Komyo Zen-in, Tofuku-
ji, Kyoto)

PLATE 106.   Pond rockwork. The scattered rocks in the pond fan out in dotted lines
from the front of the triplet rockwork. They are placed in a linear arrangement to
present a finely ordered composition. (Komyo Zen-in, Tofuku-ji, Kyoto)

PLATE 107. Full view of the garden. Thickly lichened hillocks, pure white sand, and large plantings form serene patterns. The garden, while creating a natural landscape, transcends nature to express the Zen concept. (Komyo Zen-in, Tofuku-ji, Kyoto)

PLATE 108. Bird's-eye view of the Daichi-ji garden. (Daichi-ji, Minakuchi-machi, Shiga Pref.)

PLATE 109. Turtle-shaped planting. The planting symbolizes the guardian deity of this holy precinct. (Daichi-ji, Minakuchi-machi, Shiga Pref.)

127

PLATE 110. Full-length view of the garden. The flat lichened rock in the foreground is the worship stone where priests used to sit to worship the holy images represented by the plants. Small clustered plantings among the longer wavy ones represent the seven images of Supreme Wisdom. Like the Komyo Zen-in garden this is a three-dimensional version of a painting with a triplet image of Buddha, using live plant material as the medium of expression. (Daichi-ji, Minakuchi-machi, Shiga Pref.)

PLATE 111.   Full view of the Jizo-in garden. (Jizo-in, Kyoto)

PLATE 112.   Arhat rocks. Three rocks depict Arhat's postures of standing, sitting, and reclining. The viewer senses a human quality about them. (Jizo-in, Kyoto)

PLATE 113. Arhat rocks. These mountain rocks with their lichened surfaces and sharp edges change expression with the sunlight, and the appear-
ances they present at different times of day are quite varied. (Jizo-in,
Kyoto)

PLATE 114. Standing Arhat rock. This towering rock stands majestically. The lichen covering makes it look like a figure in a priest's robe. (Jizo-in, Kyoto)

PLATE 115. Sitting Arhat rock. This rock gives a feeling of stability and quiet ease. (Jizo-in, Kyoto)

PLATE 116. Full view of the Tokai-an garden. This small courtyard garden is seen from the corridor. The rocks are arranged with good proportion and unity, regardless of the direction from which the arrangement is viewed. The angular rocks have many different planes which produce edge lines of great intricacy. (Tokai-an, Kyoto)

PLATE 117. Solar Buddha rockwork. The large rock at the left dominates the composition. Together with the other two rocks it forms a triplet rockwork. (Tokai-an, Kyoto)

PLATE 118 *(facing page)*. Full view of the rockwork. The rhythmical arrangement attracts and holds the viewer's attention. (Tokai-an, Kyoto)

132

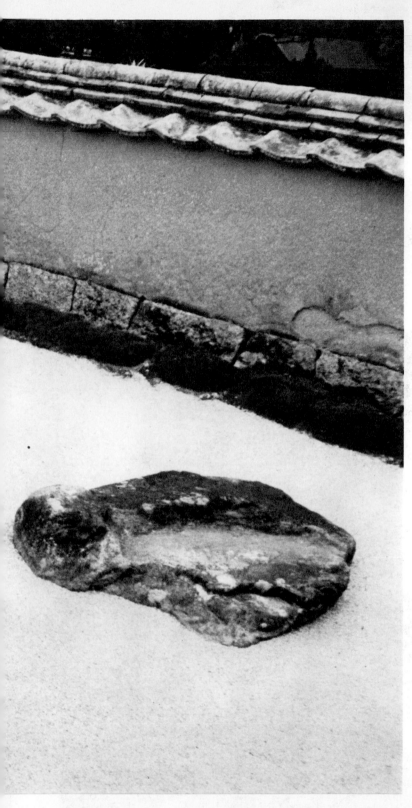

PLATE 119.   Hare and oyster rockworks in the garden of the Katsura residence. The pregnant hare rockwork is on the left and the rock of the oyster is at right. (Katsura residence, Hofu, Yamaguchi Pref.)

PLATE 120.   Panoramic view of the East and South gardens. The left portion extending to the L-shaped hare rockwork is the East Garden, and the right portion is the South Garden. The rocks in the left corner are a shade and light (*in* and *yo*) rockwork, consisting of an upright and a flat rock. In front are kei-seki. The rocks to the right and left of the L-shaped pregnant hare are representations of the oyster. The one at right is pregnant with a pearl. The South Garden symbolically expresses the world of Taoist demigods, which is composed of three gigantic mountains and ten vast seas. Three upright rocks symbolize the mountains, and white sand, the seas. In the right corner is a flat, rectangular stone representing a boat. (Katsura residence, Hofu, Yamaguchi Pref.)

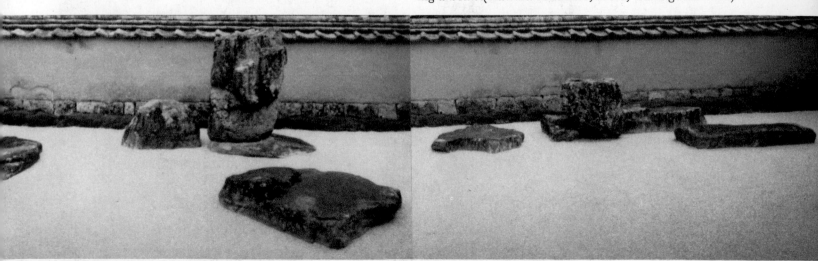

PLATE 121.   East Garden. At the back corner is the shade and light rockwork. The kei-seki rockwork is in the foreground. (Katsura residence, Hofu, Yamaguchi Pref.)

PLATE 122.   Oyster rockwork. The enlarged body reveals the shape of the pearl within it. (Katsura residence, Hofu, Yamaguchi Pref.)

PLATE 123. South Garden, the earth and the ocean (sanzan-jisshu) rockwork. (Katsura residence, Hofu, Yamaguchi Pref.)

PLATE 124. Boat stone and the earth and the ocean rockwork. (Katsura residence, Hofu, Yamaguchi Pref.)

PLATE 125. West Garden of Ryogen-in. Lichen mounds with gently undulating lines are in fine harmony with the white sand. The steppingstones of the path in the foreground enable the viewer to enjoy the garden from various directions. The triangular stone projecting from the sand sea depicts a distant mountain. (Ryogen-in, Kyoto)

PLATE 126. East Garden. The small flat stone symbolizes a raindrop which has fallen into the sea, describing circular ripples. The other rocks portray mountains. (Ryogen-in, Kyoto)

PLATE 127. Cloud patterns of the Kozen-ji garden. (Kozen-ji, Fukushima-machi, Nagano Pref.)

PLATE 128. Full view of the garden. White lines on the sand describe the shapes of clouds. The sand patterns symbolically portray cloud patterns. (Kozen-ji, Fukushima-machi, Nagano Pref.)

141

PLATE 129. East Garden. This karesansui depicts the nine mountains and eight seas of kuzan-hakkai, using Shumisen rockwork and reddish brown sand. (Ryogin-an, Kyoto)

PLATE 130. Dragon rockwork of the West Garden of Ryogin-an. The three erect edging rocks represent a dragon's head. (Ryogin-an, Kyoto)

PLATE 131. Central part of the West Garden. (Ryogin-an, Kyoto)

144

PLATE 132. West Garden and background viewed from the south. (Ryogin-an, Kyoto)

PLATE 133. Detail of sand patterns and rockwork, southwest corner of the West Garden. The rockwork gives an extremely active expression among the black clouds. (Ryogin-an, Kyoto)

PLATE 134.   Detail of sand patterns, southern corner of the West Garden. The spiral patterns describe rising black clouds with dramatic effect. (Ryogin-an, Kyoto)

PLATE 135.   Full view of the dragon rockwork, northeast corner of the West Garden.
Four elongated rocks represent the dragon's body, their edging lines undulating and
creating a feeling of movement. (Ryogin-an, Kyoto)

PLATE 136.   Detail of sand patterns, northern corner of the West
Garden. (Ryogin-an, Kyoto)

PLATE 137. Rockwork of the South Garden of Zuiho-in. A gigantic upright rock on the mossy hillock and three other rocks abstractly portray the landscape of Mt. Hyakujo. The lichened heap at the right extends to form a point of land. Rocks placed on the white sand are for scenic effect. (Zuiho-in, Daitoku-ji, Kyoto)

PLATE 138. Detail of sand patterns and a kei-seki. One scenic stone forms a distant mountain (symbol of the ideal land) and provides an accent to the expanse of white. The beauty of the plain sand background symbolizes the realm of mysticism. (Zuiho-in, Daitoku-ji, Kyoto)

PLATE 139.   Symbolic lake. Water from Mt. Hyakujo fills the lake. Formed by the deeply indented coastline, the shape of the lake resembles a starfish. The natural stone bridge at the left, which is part of the garden path, spans a valley. White sand and green moss combine to form a picturesque and abstract composition. The garden is designed so that the viewer can appreciate every part of it from the path. (Zuiho-in, Daitoku-ji, Kyoto)

PLATE 140. Detail of a section of the lake. (Zuiho-in, Daitoku-ji, Kyoto)

PLATE 141.   Full view of the lake. (Zuiho-in, Daitoku-ji, Kyoto)

PLATE 142.   North Garden viewed from the west. (Zuiho-in, Daitoku-ji, Kyoto)

PLATE 143.   North Garden viewed from the east. (Zuiho-in, Daitoku-ji, Kyoto)

PLATE 144. Full view of the North Garden from the west. Kei-seki provide an accent to the white expanse of sand. They are arranged in line with the edge of the rock by the moss mound. The steppingstones in the foreground form a path to the teahouse at the rear. (Zuiho-in, Daitoku-ji, Kyoto)

PLATE 145. Kei-seki in the East Garden of Sangen-in. The triangular rock represents a distant mountain in an abstract manner. Other rocks are used for scenic effect. (Sangen-in, Daitoku-ji, Kyoto)

PLATE 146. Kei-seki and tree in the East Garden. The tree and variously shaped kei-seki create the appearance of a still valley. (Sangen-in, Daitoku-ji, Kyoto)

153

PLATE 147.   Full view of the East Garden to the north. Upright rocks in the rear corner form a dry waterfall. A flat white stone directly in front of the largest waterfall rock is the basin stone, which is said to weigh six metric tons; most of it is buried. All the trees behind the karataki rockwork are maple, and in autumn they inject a brilliant red into the otherwise sober color scheme of the garden. (Sangen-in, Daitoku-ji, Kyoto)

3 : "Taoist Paradise" Gardens

THERE ARE many gardens which symbolize the islands of paradise of Taoist demigod-hermits *(sennin)*, or which illustrate tales of paradise with rockworks of a crane and a turtle. This style is used not only in stone gardens but also in those that have water, and well typifies Japanese gardens.

The *Resshi,* a book of tales of paradise written around the 1st century B.C., contains the following description of the islands of paradise: "There is an ocean toward the eastern end of the earth. It is as deep as a bottomless canyon. Even the River of Heaven [the Milky Way] does not flow into this ocean; however, throughout eternity the water will neither increase nor decrease. . . . *Sennin* live together happily on these islands of everlasting spring, which produce the elixir of life." In the *Hekiganroku* it is said that in paradise, "ten thousand years . . . flies in a moment; a moment lingers like ten thousand years. Forests of coral overgrow this eternal land." According to another ancient book on mythology, "These islands yield jewelry and incense and their wonder-working springs splash and ripple. They command magnificent views of rivers and mountains in an eternal spring with neither immoderate heat nor cold." The world here described is Utopia.

In the Orient, particularly in Japan, gardens are regarded not simply as objects of aesthetic appreciation but as protectors of the families who have them, a concept that came to Japan from ancient China. Gardens are thought to bring prosperity, peace, and good health, and they are treated as a living prayer for the family's long life. To create in a garden the eternal spring of paradise expresses the desire to attain paradise after death. People might also be motivated to make this kind of garden by the wish to render their lives more pleasant by having their *sennin* close at hand in rock form.

Both the crane and the turtle have traditionally been regarded as symbols of long life and protection of the family. The ancient people of the East believed that the turtle was the holy creature who supports the world on its back. Thus the rock arrangement of a turtle in a garden represents protection from natural disasters and proper control of rivers. The crane is also regarded as a holy creature and was thought to trans-

155

port the demigod-hermits from one place to another. Both animals functioned as fetishes. Taoist gardens have a definite aura of Oriental mystery, a rather romantic quality of Japan.

Tofuku-ji

Plates 148–153
Figure 37
■ The stone garden of this temple is built around the hall. Each part (north, south, east, and west) is designed differently, but all are modern in concept. The South Garden, the largest of the four, performs the leading role. It is a model of the islands of paradise. Figure 37 well illustrates the composition: three huge oblong rocks, and several towering crags around each of them, are arranged to form the three islands. At their right, an enormous upright rock is arranged with five smaller stones around it to form another island. These sacred islands, four in all, are surrounded by whirlpool-patterned sand. The rockworks confront one another with sharp edges expressing an intense rhythm overflowing with dynamic movement, similar to the Stoic manners of Rinzai's Zen.

The West Garden contains a neat rural landscape arranged with finely pruned azaleas. The North Garden has an abstract, geometric composition similar to that of a Mondrian painting; it combines square flat rocks with moss. The East Garden employs columnar foundation stones to represent a Great Bear in the sand pattern. Located in Kyoto, the gardens were designed in 1939 by Mirei Shigemori and cover an area of 10,480 square feet.

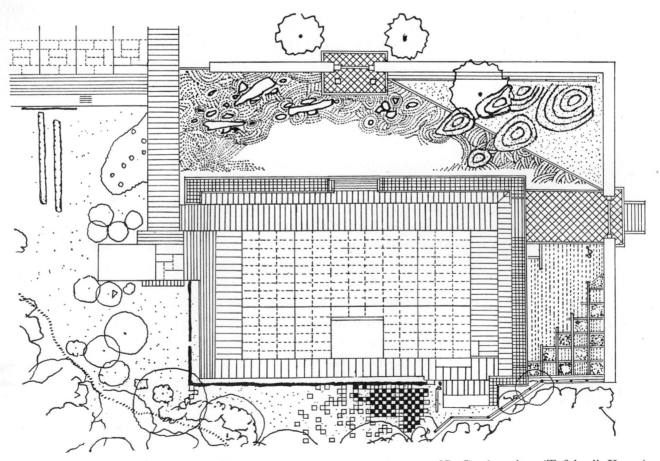

FIG. 37. Garden plan. (Tofuku-ji, Kyoto)

FIG. 38. Konchi-in garden. (Konchi-in, Nanzen-ji, Kyoto)

Konchi-in

Plates 154–158

Figure 38

■ This noted stone garden is the widest of all the classical ones depicting paradise. The landscape is composed of the paradise rockwork in the center with the crane and turtle on either side. Four islands depicting paradise are constructed on black pebbles, and low rockwork represents background scenery. In front of the paradise rockwork is laid a huge, rectangular slab of rock, a natural stone five feet by thirteen. This is the boat stone on which Abbot Suden (head of the nation's religious administration in the 17th century) formerly sat and worshiped at the Toshogu Shrine. The shrine was dedicated to Ieyasu Tokugawa, founder of the Edo shogunate (which lasted for 264 years beginning in 1603), and was built over his grave. Located at Nanzen-ji, Kyoto, the garden was designed by Enshu Kobori and Kentei in 1633. It has an area of 53,262 square feet.

Raikyu-ji

Plates 159–163

Figure 39

■ In this garden, islands of the crane and the turtle surrounded by wave-patterned azaleas create the Taoist paradise. The large azalea plants form a background of great beauty, as well as symbolizing the clean and peaceful state of mind of Zen enlightenment. The viewer is particularly attracted by the aesthetic composition of the crane rockwork. Concentrating on the upright rock at the center, one can see that this rockwork abstractly depicts a crane's splendid figure. Azaleas around the rocks give the impression that the bird must be large and gorgeous. The garden was designed by Enshu Kobori in the early 17th century and is located in Takahashi, Okayama Prefecture. Its area is 6,994 square feet.

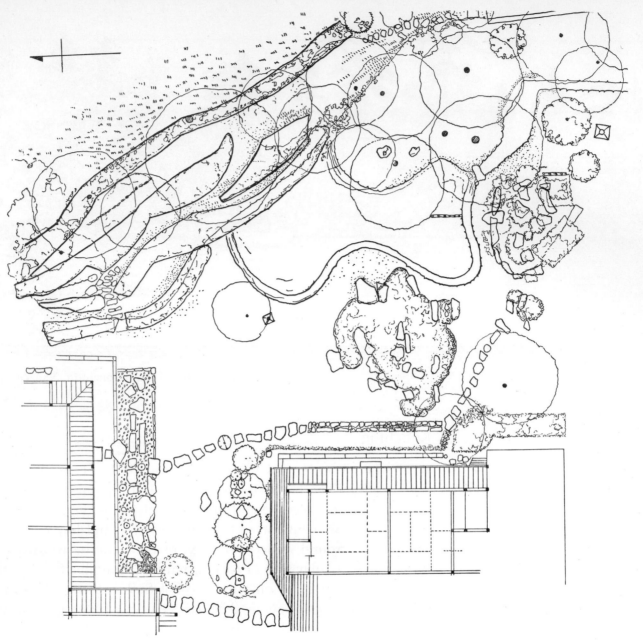

FIG. 39. Garden plan. (Raikyu-ji, Takahashi, Okayama Pref.)

Sesshu-ji

Plates 164–166 ■ A 17th-century book on landscape architecture contains the following instructions: "Build an island in the center of the garden. This stands for Mt. Horai [a holy mountain which gives the elixir of life]. Its shape resembles that of a turtle. Therefore, it should have a head-rock, limb-rocks, and a tail-rock. These are absolutely necessary. In addition, it is indispensable to plant a pine tree on the back, or else to erect a rock as a substitute for the pine."

The turtle island of the Sesshu-ji garden adheres to the design described above. At its right, the rockwork of the crane island is arranged to complete the holy pair. The tall rock in the form of a crane firmly rests on a moss groundcover; it is appropriate as a fetish symbolizing peace, eternal youth, and happiness. Built in Kyoto during the 16th century, the garden is 2,152 square feet. Its designer is unknown.

COLOR PLATE 3 *(facing page).* Tofuku-ji, Kyoto

PLATE 149. Full view of the South Garden. The three islands are composed of huge oblong and towering craggy rocks. In the far corner moss mounds depict the five holy mountains in miniature. (Tofuku-ji, Kyoto)

163

PLATE 150. Full view of the West Garden. The squarely trimmed azaleas form a balanced geometric composition. (Tofuku-ji, Kyoto)

PLATE 151. West Garden viewed from the south. A triplet rockwork is shown in the foreground. (Tofuku-ji, Kyoto)

164

PLATE 152. North Garden. Square flagstones are inlaid among masses of thick green moss. The spatial composition has static balance and geometric beauty. (Tofuku-ji, Kyoto)

PLATE 153.   Great bear rockwork in the East Garden. The seven columnar stones of various heights are rhythmically arranged. These stones were waste materials salvaged from the foundation of a ruined building, demonstrating that a fine aesthetic effect can be achieved in a stone garden with the simplest of materials. (Tofuku-ji, Kyoto)

166

PLATE 154. Central part of the Konchi-in garden. The islands of paradise are set behind the rectangular worship stone in the center foreground. Scenic stones are arranged to form a miniature landscape on a hill. Sheared plantings in the background depict a deep mountain ravine. (Konchi-in, Nanzen-ji, Kyoto)

PLATE 155. Turtle-island rockwork. The turtle-shaped hill with an old pine tree on its back forms Mt. Horai ("mountain of lotus flowers" in Sanskrit and also a name for turtle). The presence of the pine tree symbolizes the turtle's shouldering the weight of the world. The turtle's head is at the left. (Konchi-in, Nanzen-ji, Kyoto)

PLATE 156. The islands of paradise. The islands form a line which runs from the crane to the turtle. On small dark stones are placed the white, black, and bluish green island-rocks. Esteemed for their rarity, these materials are all mountain rocks. (Konchi-in, Nanzen-ji, Kyoto)

PLATE 157. Crane-island rockwork. The rocks, most of which are in an upright position, are beautifully grouped. Though not as concrete a representation as the turtle island, it gives the impression of a crane's form. This rockwork is similar in beauty to a Japanese bridal costume which has been skillfully made. (Konchi-in, Nanzen-ji, Kyoto)

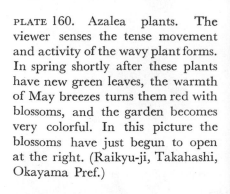

PLATE 158. Steppingstones. These famous steppingstones form an arc which is called the Great Curve. The path describes a 45-degree parabola and connects with the walk of the Toshogu Shrine. The arrangement of square stone slabs, which are laid alternately straight and on end, creates a novel pattern. (Konchi-in, Nanzen-ji, Kyoto)

PLATE 159. Full view of the Raikyu-ji garden. The garden incorporates a distant mountain as part of the scenery. The mountain blends perfectly with this paradise garden, which thus becomes one with nature. (Raikyu-ji, Takahashi, Okayama Pref.)

PLATE 160. Azalea plants. The viewer senses the tense movement and activity of the wavy plant forms. In spring shortly after these plants have new green leaves, the warmth of May breezes turns them red with blossoms, and the garden becomes very colorful. In this picture the blossoms have just begun to open at the right. (Raikyu-ji, Takahashi, Okayama Pref.)

PLATE 161. Crane-island rockwork and azalea plants. The azaleas surge in five grand curves, which give a sublime form to the garden. (Raikyu-ji, Takahashi, Okayama Pref.)

PLATE 162. Full view of the crane island. The flapping crane stands like a queen: azaleas form her wings, and the erect rock in the center her head and neck. The crest of the mountain in the background echoes the lines of the standing rock, creating a subtle and unified composition. (Raikyu-ji, Takahashi, Okayama Pref.)

PLATE 163.   View from the window at Raikyu-ji. The inlaid stone slabs and large sheared plantings are seen from the round window. (Raikyu-ji, Takahashi, Okayama Pref.)

are the stone basin, lantern, and a bamboo tube which drips water, producing intermittent sounds *(sozu)*. There is a wide variation in the appearance of stone accessories, for they can be natural rocks, stones which have been cut to order, millstones, foundation stones, or other previously used stones. All garden accessories are placed near the path which runs from the gate to the teahouse.

Kanden-an

Plates 168–171
Figure 40

■ This typical tea garden makes good use of elements which are practical as well as decorative in the design of the steppingstones and pavements. The path takes the guest from the steppingstones at the garden gate to a pavement of small round and rectangularly cut stones; then, by way of other steppingstones, it extends to a stone pavement edged with bamboo poles and to more steppingstones which lead to the entrance of the teahouse. The composition of this garden path arranged on red sand demonstrates the beautiful decorative quality of the flat stones, which present pictorial patterns. The pavement with bamboo edges is conspicuously creative and original, indicating the taste and artistry of the garden's owner. New green poles are set in place for every tea ceremony; the contrast of the bamboo with the red sand and brown mountain-stone pavement creates a fresh yet calm atmosphere which provides a respite from civilization's din. When a guest walks on the pavement, he feels somewhat as though he were walking on air and feels refreshed. Designed by Fumai Matsudaira, the 18th-century lord of Matsue Castle and a noted administrator, the garden was constructed in 1790. It has an area of 5,380 square feet and is located in Matsue, Shimane Prefecture.

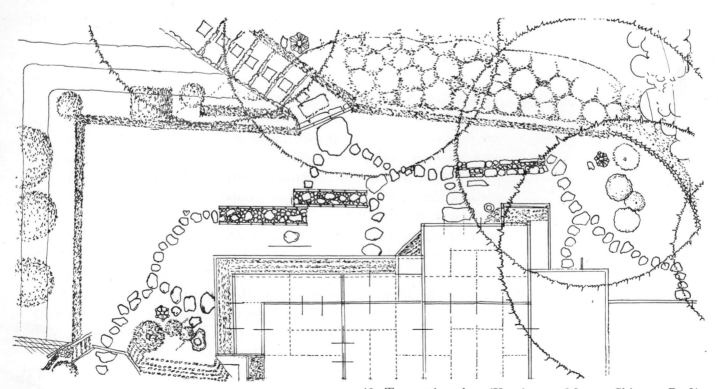

FIG. 40. Tea-garden plan. (Kanden-an, Matsue, Shimane Pref.)

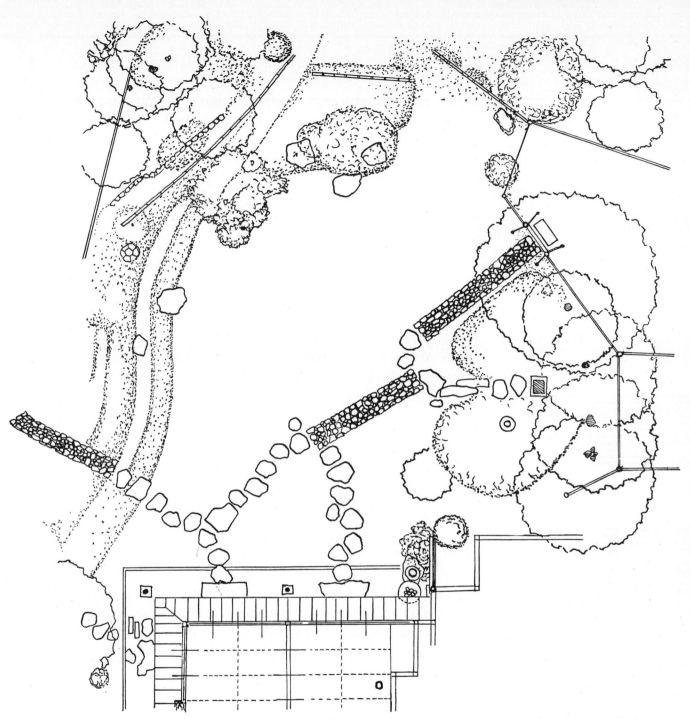

FIG. 41. Tea-garden plan. (Kokoku-ji, Hirata, Shimane Pref.)

Kokoku-ji

Plate 172
Figure 41

■ The pattern of the steppingstones and pavements of this garden is dynamic and unrestrained. Round stones split in half form the pavement. Large round steppingstones set deep as though rooted in the ground have a majestic appearance. The stones are defined against white sand in beautiful abstract patterns. This tea garden also exemplifies the highly sought quality of blending with nature. Designed by the Zen priest Toko, the garden was constructed in 1830 in Hirata, Shimane Prefecture. Its area is 8,608 square feet.

Tenju-an

Plates 173–175
Figure 42

■ This garden has a very modern design in which potentially monotonous, square-cut flagstones are transformed into a vari-patterned pavement. Raked sand represents a stream, giving a calm and composed feeling to the garden. Two round moss mounds on the sand and rocks placed under the plants at the right form a fine miniature dry landscape garden. A viewer looking at this miniature landscape from the path has a feeling of relaxation which prepares him for the fullest enjoyment of the tea ceremony. It was constructed in Kyoto in 1905, but its designer is unknown.   The garden is only 753 square feet in area.

Koho-an

Plates 176–178

■ The principal purpose of this tea garden, designed as a miniature landscape around the garden path, is aesthetic appreciation. Viewed from the window of the teahouse it has a trim appearance. The garden was designed in 1793 by Enshu Kobori and is located in Kyoto. It has an area of 4,304 square feet.

Shisendo Retreat

Plates 179, 180

■ This small garden covering the south and front areas of Shisendo was built as a retreat for the noted sinologist Jozan Ishikawa (1583–1672). It is a very beautiful garden in excellent, restrained taste. Large pruned azaleas form a miniature landscape in the South Garden. The white sand in the foreground produces a sense of quiet; sunlight sparkles on it through the leaves of the trees, and when the leaves fall they too reflect the light. Poems seem to be written on a page of white sand. When the guest looks at the garden while sipping a cup of tea he experiences a peaceful state of mind: this is the beauty of the tea garden. Designed by Jozan Ishikawa himself, the garden was constructed in Kyoto in 1641. Its area is 4,304 square feet.

Sampo-in

Plate 181
Figure 43

■ The design of this garden is achieved by defining moss forms against white sand; this produces a composition of simplicity and magnificence. The main garden is a vast, pond-inlet one, where feudal lords held cherry-blossom viewing parties, and in a corner is the teahouse to which this small tea garden is attached. The scenery of this karesansui takes the form of gourdlike saké containers with saké cups represented in abstract patterns of moss. These uniquely Japanese forms possess a feeling of weight and stability and emphasize the beauty of the moss. In contrast to the preceding gardens, this was made for aesthetic appreciation only; it is, however, a style well worthy of attention. The garden was constructed in Kyoto in 1910, but the designer is unknown. Its area is 1,614 square feet.

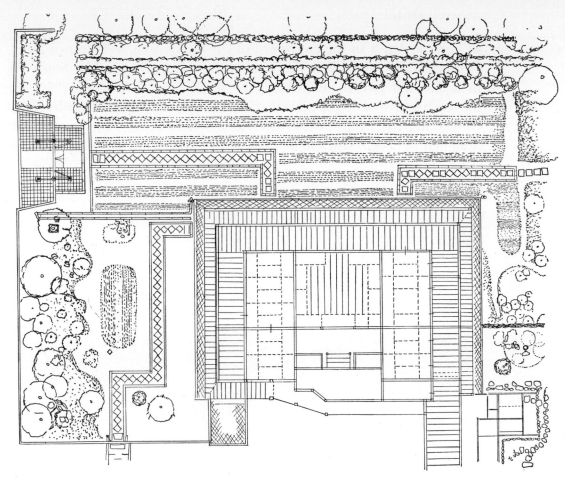

FIG. 42. Tea-garden plan. (Tenju-an, Nanzen-ji, Kyoto)

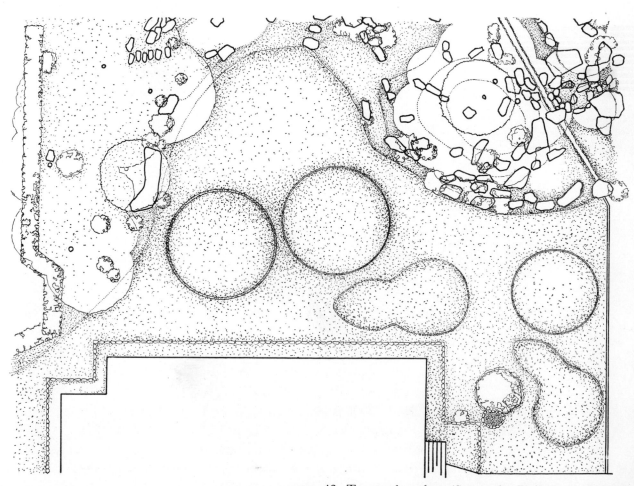

FIG. 43. Tea-garden plan. (Sampo-in, Daikaku-ji, Kyoto)

Miyako Hotel

Plates 182–184 ■ This garden is in the courtyard of the annex to a well-known hotel. It successfully reproduces the plan of the Sampo-in garden. Since the moss has not grown sufficiently, the stability of form created by the moss patterns is not yet apparent. Steppingstones form a garden path connecting the wings of the hotel. Located in Kyoto, the garden was designed by Togo Murano in 1959. It has an area of 5,380 square feet.

PLATE 167.   Front yard of Komyo Zen-in. The tea-garden style is adopted for the front yard. Cut flagstones with a geometric pattern are used for the path. Several scenic rocks by the entrance and another around the corner of the path are placed to accent space in this large garden. (Komyo Zen-in, Tofuku-ji, Kyoto)

PLATE 168. Nobedan of the Kanden-an garden. The flagstones of the pavement are interspersed with larger stones to ensure safe footing. The green bamboo poles have a striking appearance next to the dark red sand. Their color helps the garden viewer watch where he is going so that he will not wander off the pavement. The nobedan is a good example of the blending of practical and aesthetic elements. (Kanden-an, Matsue, Shimane Pref.)

181

PLATE 169. Full view of the garden. The varied composition of the stone pavement combined with the steppingstones forms an interesting pattern. (Kanden-an, Matsue, Shimane Pref.)

PLATE 170. Path's branching stones and nobedan. The larger flat stones among the steppingstones are placed at certain points so that one may branch off from the main path. (Kanden-an, Matsue, Shimane Pref.)

PLATE 172. Central part of the Kokoku-ji garden. The path of steppingstones and stone pavement extends to the teahouse inside the bamboo fence. In the background are pruned plantings of osmanthus and purple magnolia. (Kokoku-ji, Hirata, Shimane Pref.)

PLATE 171 *(facing page)*. Side view of nobedan with steppingstones behind. The flat stones are arranged beautifully in an abstract pattern. (Kanden-an, Matsue, Shimane Pref.)

PLATE 174.   Southern part of the garden. In the background are pruned azaleas. The pattern raked on the white sand expresses flowing water. (Tenju-an, Nanzen-ji, Kyoto)

PLATE 173 *(facing page)*.   Flagstone pavement of Tenju-an garden. Square-cut granite flagstones are arranged in a fresh, animated pattern. (Tenju-an, Nanzen-ji, Kyoto)

PLATE 175.   Eastern part of the garden. A white sand stream flows close to the path, creating a peaceful atmosphere. (Tenju-an, Nanzen-ji, Kyoto)

PLATE 176. Koho-an garden viewed from the west. The shoji slides up to open, presenting a view of the stone water basin and lantern with a triangular kei-seki behind them. (Koho-an, Kyoto)

PLATE 177. View of the garden from a southern window. The stone basin is in the shape of an ancient Chinese copper coin. The lantern in the background is in the oribe style. (Koho-an, Kyoto)

PLATE 178.   General view of the West Garden. The steppingstone
path incorporates the small stone bridge in the background. Pruned
azaleas at the rear represent mountain ranges and give a feeling of
serenity to the garden. (Koho-an, Kyoto)

PLATE 179. Front yard of the Shisendo Retreat. The stone pavement gently curves from the gate to the entrance. The fine composition of this pavement and steppingstones against the white sand produces a world of solitude, and the garden requires no other decoration. (Shisendo Retreat, Kyoto)

PLATE 180. General view of the southern garden. Five azalea clusters represent mountains. When they are all in bloom in spring they change the garden to scarlet. Even the white sand looks pink then, reflecting the color of the blossoms. Elegant simplicity is the impression conveyed by this garden. (Shisendo Retreat, Kyoto)

190

PLATE 181. Central view of the Sampo-in garden. The moss mound in the foreground is formed in a gourd shape, while the other mound in the background is in the shape of a saké cup. (Sampo-in, Daikaku-ji, Kyoto)

PLATE 182. Miyako Hotel tea garden viewed from the north. (Miyako Hotel, Kyoto)

PLATE 183. Tea garden seen from the south. The rock formation in the background represents a natural cliff. (Miyako Hotel, Kyoto)

193

PLATE 184.   Full view of the tea garden. (Miyako Hotel, Kyoto)

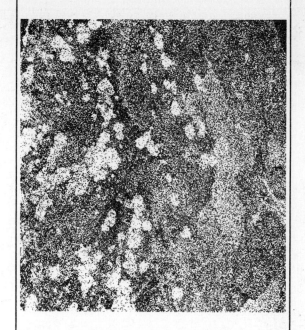

PART TWO

■

Making a
Stone Garden

造
園

5 : Rock Selection & Arrangement

Figures 44–46, (59) HAVING studied various types of Japanese stone gardens in Part One, let us now consider the requirements for making an excellent traditional one. The following points should be kept in mind: 1) No rock in a stone garden is placed on the ground but should be two-thirds buried and one-third exposed. It must be rooted in order to extend the edging lines at ground level to look like a natural outcrop. A rock which appears to have a much greater surface area showing than is needed looks as if it were afloat and is regarded as having had unrefined placement. 2) Rocks used in a stone garden are generally not quarried, nor do they have a manufactured or sculptured look because the inherent beauty of naturalness is sought. The material of a single garden is unified because a diversity of rock types would spoil the garden's refinement. 3) The direction of a rock's ridges and lines—the rock's vigor—is aesthetically appreciated and utilized in arrangement. Edges and lines are indispensable in grouping and composing the garden. 4) A rock is given life only by other rocks—it is not touched by mortar or concrete in any form. No human touches should be added; polishing with oil or water or adding coloring are practices to be completely avoided. With the passage of time rocks weather naturally, exposing a beautiful natural patina.

Selection

Rock materials for the garden are found on mountains, the seashore, and in rivers. It is necessary to distinguish between the exposed and buried parts of the stones as they will appear in the finished garden, and rocks are chosen according to their use in the composition. They should have a hard texture and dark tone, such as black, green, brown, or gray. White or other tones close to primary colors should be avoided, as should lustrous rocks, such as marble.

Fine-grained granite rocks, with rusty tones of brown and dark green, are generally used in Japanese stone gardens. These are mostly fine-grained biotite granite and diorite proper. Others are andesitic or basaltic rocks, such as enstatite andesite, two-pyroxene andesite, glassy

FIG. 44. Basic parts of a rock: A) head; B) body; C) hips; D) foot.

Plates (12–17, 37–41, 50–53, 90–94) biotite andesite, olivine basalt, dolerite, hornblende-quartz basalt, etc. Particularly in Kyoto there are a number of stone gardens which use diorite proper in their rockwork arrangements. Of the metamorphic rocks, types of crystalline schist, such as dark piedmontite and chlorite schist, are used. For a *karataki-ishi* rhyolite is used. For master and scenic rocks, metamorphic schistose rocks are often chosen. Chlorite schist is especially prized and appreciated in Japanese gardens; called green rock, it is used to symbolize a towering mountain. (See plates for Ogawa residence, Kanji-in, Fukuda residence, Kishiwada Castle gardens.)

When selected for gardens, rocks are classified according to their place of origin. Some are weathered by oxygen from the air, some are eroded by water, and others are changed in structure by the internal movements of the earth. Thus the garden-maker must consider which rocks should be used where, according to their classification:

1. *Mountain rock.* This type of rock has been transformed by accumulations of earth. The exposed part used for the stone garden is a rusty or blackish brown as a result of weathering, and the edges are made smooth and round by this same process. The buried parts of these rocks, however, retain their fresh texture. This type of rock generally serves as a supplementary or accompanying one placed near the master rock. Sometimes, however, a rock with a widely exposed section is used for the master rock itself.

2. *Valley rock.* *Sawa-ishi* is the Japanese term for this type of rock— originally mountain rock—found in the rapids or by a valley stream. However, it has not been affected much by the water current, and its surface is not very worn. Unlike mountain rock it has not become rust colored from weathering. It retains a moderately round shape, and one can find valley rocks with beautiful lines. This type, usually a phyllite, such as chlorite schist or piedmontite schist, is considered best for rock arrangements, and most Japanese stone gardens use *sawa-ishi*.

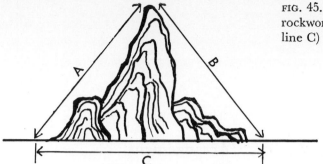

FIG. 45. Width and vigor of the rockwork. A three-piece rockwork has two vigorous lines A) and B) and a horizontal line C) representing the width.

FIG. 46. Directions of rock vigor. The vigor is indicated by arrows, its direction being determined by the angle of the rock's head.

3. *River rock.* This type is well eroded by the rapid current of a river. It has such a round, smooth surface caused by friction with other stones and water that it scarcely blends with other rock material for arrangements and is usually used for flagstones or steppingstones. Severely eroded rocks with depressions or cavities are used for water basins.

4. *Marine rock.* This is rock weathered by the sea. Originally from mountains, storms and floods carried these rocks down to the seashore. There they were eroded by the ocean into the shape of an outcrop with a very smooth, round surface. Marine rocks are not generally used in gardens, except for gigantic eroded ones sometimes used independently to represent an object or compose a miniature island.

5. *Water stone.* The proper use of water stones is in *bonseki,* a miniature landscape stone laid on a tray, and not in traditional stone gardens. These are valley stones taken from river beds. The dealers who handle water stones *(sui-seki)* often change the shape of the stones somewhat by grinding and polishing them with oil to fully bring out the color and sheen.

Of the five types mentioned above, mountain and valley rocks are most used in garden arrangements. In the case of both, a rock having a hard, smooth texture and well-rounded shape is considered best. Rocks having linear and sharply angular edges are avoided, except when used as a scenic stone or *karataki.* Regarding color, the rocks used should be of a dark or rusty hue which shows the iron content, giving a subtle tone together with a feeling of weight and solidity. (See Table 1, p. 210.)

Arrangement

For many generations in the Orient, rocks and stones have been aesthetically arranged to compose the rock groupings of karesansui. Various methods of arrangement have been transmitted over time. As is illustrated by the gardens considered in Part One, the basic composition of rocks is the most important factor in the creation of a beautiful stone garden. In Japanese landscaping terminology the verbs "place," "pile," and "arrange" are not used to describe the handling of rocks; instead, "combine," "imbed," "sink," and "root" describe the process. The use of the latter terms indicates that the garden-maker handles rocks in the closest relationship with the environment in which they are placed.

Figure 47   Figure 47 shows the basic rock shapes. The master rock A) has the most important role in an arrangement. This upright rock must have a form which looks dignified and majestic. B) is called a "pillar rock" because of its shape; also known as "body rock," it is an important component of a *karataki* rockwork. C) is called "branch rock" and is used as a supplementary or accompanying rock or as a scenic one if placed alone. D), a semiflat rock having the shape of a reclining ox, is used as a scenic rock or a dead (inactive) stone setting off other stones. It is also used as the supplementary or accompanying rock for an upright master rock. E) is a flat rock providing a place to worship or burn incense. This type combined with an upright rock symbolizes the balance of dark and light (Japanese *in* and *yo*) elements of the universe. It is also used to compose a miniature mountain range with a single rock as the scenic material. These five rock shapes may be used in five basic combinations, as shown in Figures 48 to 54. These are described below:

Plate (84)   1. *One-piece rockwork.* A single rock is placed as a scenic rock or inactive stone to fill a space. A mountain, range of mountains, or an island may also be represented with a single rock. Because each rock has its own particular shape the garden-maker can depict a miniature mountain by selecting a triangular-shaped rock resembling a distant mountain, while for another purpose he may select a heavy rock with fine balance. If a rock is placed as a scenic accent to be viewed from all directions, it must have good lines and angles on all sides; if it is to be seen from one side, a fairly thick schistose rock is best. The most important factor in placing a scenic or inactive stone is to make sure that the stone actually works as an accent within that space: the stone should be the focal point of the space, controlling the tensions surrounding it. Plate 84 provides a good example of such a rock placement.

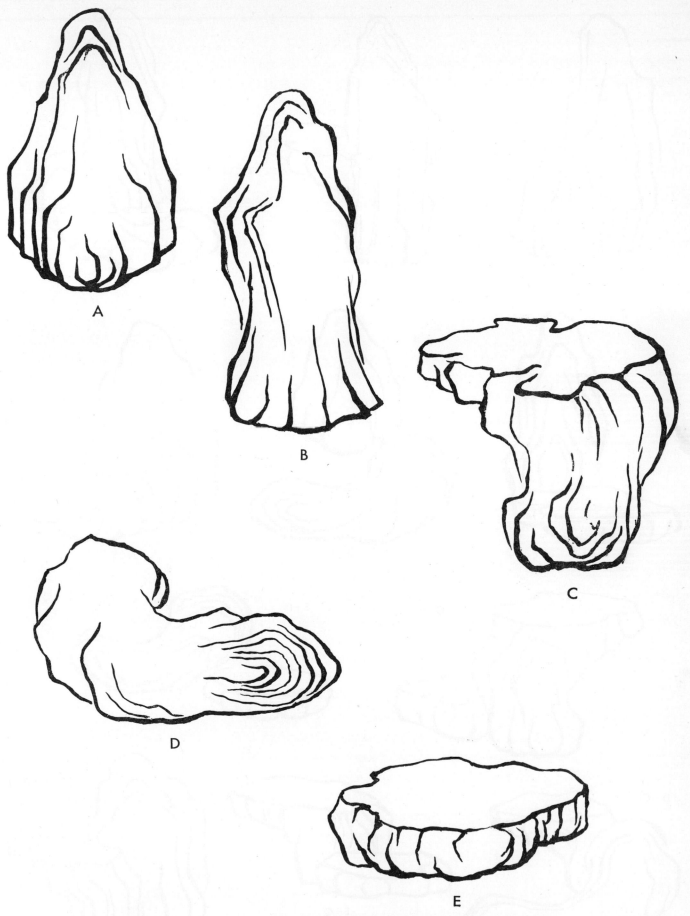

FIG. 47. The five basic rock shapes: A) master rock; B) pillar rock; C) branch rock; D) semiflat rock; E) flat rock.

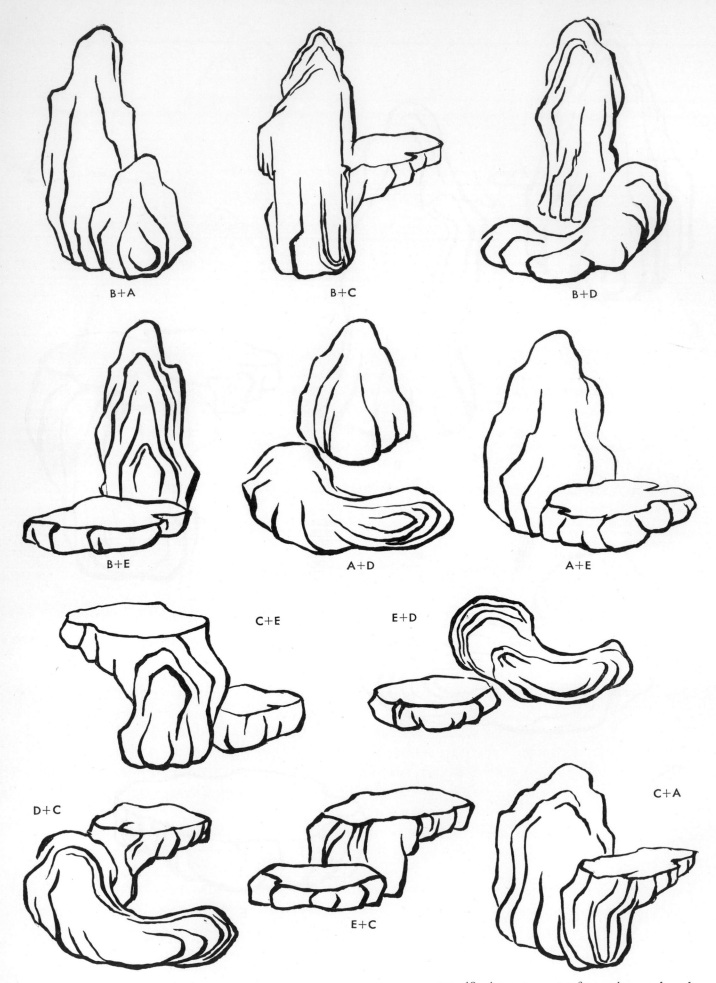

B+A

B+C

B+D

B+E

A+D

A+E

C+E

E+D

D+C

E+C

C+A

FIG. 48. Arrangements of two-piece rockwork.

FIG. 49. Basic forms of two-piece rockwork, a master rock and an accompanying rock in perspective.

FIG. 50. Basic forms of two-piece rockwork, viewed from a different angle.

Figures 48–50   2. *Two-piece rockwork*. Arrangements with two or any even number of rocks are not usually made. Thus the two-piece rockwork belongs to a special grouping which is regarded as a single unit composed of two parts. In the two-piece rockworks of Figures 49 and 50, one rock functions as the principal and the other as a subordinate or supplementary rock. A combination of two rocks of equal balance is never desirable since aesthetics require that proportional relationships of height, width, and depth be keenly integrated. The rockwork that looks longer horizontally is in better taste than one composed with a strong vertical line; this means that the edges of the rocks should be arranged to expand the lines in width. The distance between the two rocks should be of moderate proportion and length, not too far and not too close. This must be dealt with case by case because of the nature of rock shapes used. In any event, however, the subordinate rock must be placed within the area which the master rock controls—the subordinate rock must be seen as the spatial extension of the force of the master rock.

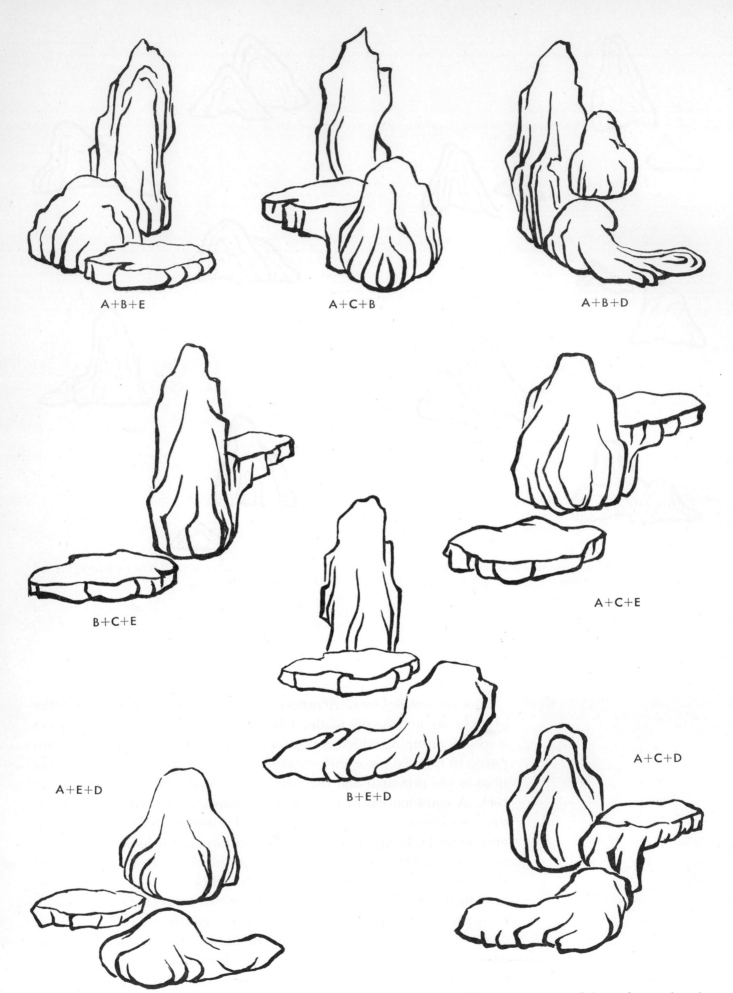

A+B+E

A+C+B

A+B+D

B+C+E

A+C+E

A+E+D

B+E+D

A+C+D

FIG. 51. Arrangements of three-piece rockwork.

FIG. 52. Basic forms of the three-piece rockwork, master rock and two accompanying rocks.

FIG. 53. Basic forms of the three-piece rockwork, large, medium, and small-sized rocks.

Figures 51–53

3. *Three-piece rockwork.* The three-piece rockwork is the most typical of all the various styles of rock arrangement, and other rockworks of odd numbers are formed on the basis of the three-piece rockwork pattern. The number three has been traditionally associated in Japan and China with infinity and is fundamental in Japanese aesthetics. It is regarded as mystic and sacred, comparable to the trinity of Christianity. The *sanzon-seki* rockwork, for example, simulates the three holy images of Buddhist painting, and the dry waterfall rockwork is also composed of three rocks.

The basic composition of the three-piece rockwork is the combination of one-to-two: a master rock and two accompanying rocks (Fig. 52). In this composition the two small rocks make the base of the master rock appear to expand widely, giving an impression of greater volume. The perspective created by different intervals of space between the rocks brings out various aspects of the master rock. Thus the line produced by the rockwork can run in any direction one wishes.

The other principal method of combining three rocks is the combination of one large, one medium, and one small rock (Fig. 53). In this arrangement the large rock is the master or host rock, the medium-sized rock is the guest rock, and the smallest is the accompanying rock.

FIG. 54. Example of a completed rockwork combining two- and three-piece rockworks.

The host rock should be an upright form, the guest rock a flat form, and the accompanying rock a smaller upright shape. The master rock must show strong spirit and express a regal appearance. The guest rock functions to acknowledge the primacy of the master rock and heightens the beauty of the latter through its placement nearby. The accompanying rock supplements the appearance of the other two rocks in a reserved manner.

In either method of arrangement the master rock's make-up should be expressed in the best possible manner by utilizing linear and angular elements. The garden-maker must seek a unified effect rather than the effect of any individual rock within the group. An organic combination of the three is required to obtain harmony, balance, and beauty.

Figures 54–56   4. *Five-piece rockwork*. There are five categories of proportions for the five-piece rockwork which are all derived from the basic three-piece rockwork (Figs. 54–56). These are described below:

a) Three-to-two. The basic form is a three-piece rockwork with two supplementary rocks added. The supplementary rocks give the three-piece rockwork the appearance of having a broader base.

b) Four-to-one. There are few examples of this type. The basic form is a composition of two groupings of two rocks each, linked by a supplementary rock. The other form is composed with a large master rock and four supplementary rocks.

c) Three-to-one-to-one. This type of rockwork resembles the three-to-two rockwork except that the two rocks work independently on the three-piece rockwork.

d) Two-to-two-to-one. In this type two groupings of two rocks each are arranged with a supplementary rock between them. Although very similar to the four-to-one rockwork, the supplementary rock of this type is treated as an organic unit in itself.

e) One-to-one-to-three. This type forms a very irregular appearance centering on the master rock; four supplementary rocks cluster near it.

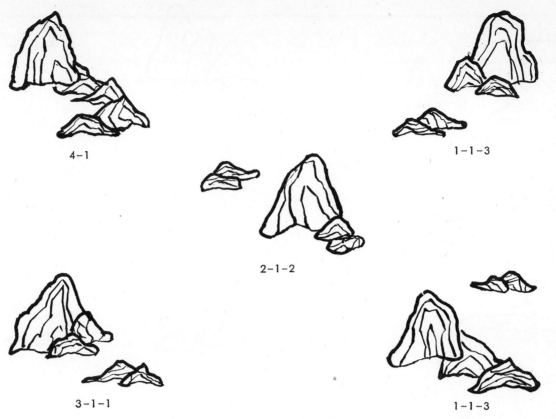

FIG. 55. Three variations of the five-piece rock-work: 4–1; 2–1–2 or 2–3; 1–1–3, 3–1–1, and 1–1–3.

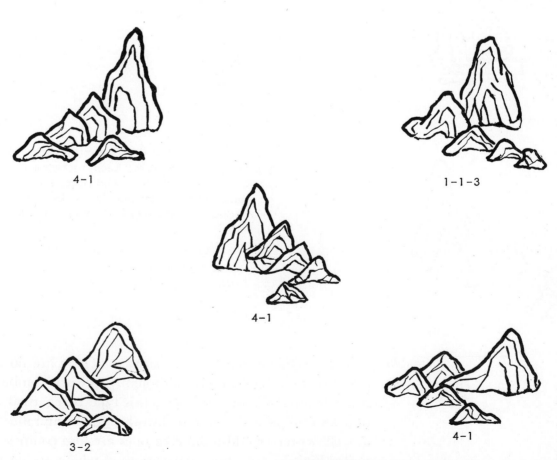

FIG. 56. Variations of the five-piece rockwork: 4–1, 1–1–3 or 2–3, 4–1, 3–2, and 4–1.

FIG. 57. Basic forms of the seven-piece rockwork, a three-piece and two two-piece rockworks. Each rockwork comprises a mountain range with a craggy ridge. The larger the master rock the greater the number of the accompanying rocks and the deeper and wider the appearance of the rockwork, which give a fine perspective.

Plate (98)

Figures 57, 58

5. *Seven-piece and nine-piece rockworks.* (There are no rockworks composed of six or eight rocks; although rockwork combining two three-piece groupings totals six rocks, this type is regarded as a compound unit and not as a six-piece rockwork.) Seven- and nine-piece rockwork as well as greater odd-numbered ones are also composed of compound units (Figs. 57, 58), the compositions of which are developed from the basic rockwork compositions just described. The famous rockwork of

FIG. 58. Variations of the nine-piece rockwork. Considerably more complicated than the seven-piece rockwork, this type has variety of form and requires great skill in composition. There are many variations; seven-, five-, and three-piece rockworks may be combined with a nine-piece one to create a magnificent and balanced design of compound units.

Ryoan-ji depicting a mountain view is a good example showing the three-piece rockwork as the basis of composition (Plate 98). The basic form of this "aesthetic triangle" is seen not only in the stone garden but also in the landscape painting of medieval Japan and China. Systematic composition of rockwork is the aesthetic basis of the Japanese stone garden, in which the spatial relationships create beauty of corresponding and responding forms.

Group	Name	Color	Use in rockwork
Igneous rock	fine-grained biotite granite	gray	master rocks
	enstatite andesite	dark gray	master and scenic rocks
	two-pyroxene andesite	greenish black	master and scenic rocks
	glassy biotite andesite	dark brown	master and scenic rocks
	olivine basalt	gray	master and scenic rocks
	dolerite proper	dark green	master and scenic rocks
	diorite proper	dark brown	master and scenic rocks
	rhyolite	dark brown	master and scenic rocks
	enstatolite	black	master and scenic rocks
	hornblende-quartz basalt	dark gray	master and scenic rocks
Metamorphic rock	chlorite schist	dark green	scenic rocks
	epidote schist	gray-blue	scenic rocks
	anthophyllite schist	gray-brown	scenic rocks
	hematite-quartz schist	dark brown	scenic rocks
	mica quartz schist	gray	scenic rocks
	biotite schist	dark brown	scenic rocks
	granite gneiss	gray-brown	scenic rocks
	sandstone hornfels	brown	scenic rocks
	piedmontite schist	brown	scenic rocks
	actinolite schist	brown	pavement stone, for use in *nobedan* only
	amphibole schist	brown	pavement stone, for use in *nobedan* only

6 : Construction & Spacing

Construction of Rockwork

The Western garden-maker will be able to create a stone garden in the Japanese style only if he has basic, practical knowledge of its construction. However, special technical skill is not required although some technical matters are involved. Of primary importance is the placement of the rocks to show their surface from the most effective direction. This is achieved by exploiting the vigor of the rocks, for they possess great natural beauty when the vigor of edging lines is well expressed.

Rocks must be buried, which is called "rooting" in the technical terminology of stone gardening. Naturally there is a maximum depth desirable for rooting, but its purpose is to make the exposed part of the rock look stable, as though it were a natural outcrop. The appearance of being separate from the ground—of being afloat—must be avoided at all times in the placement of rocks. When a rock is placed in an upright position, it must be deeply rooted to appear firmly settled. If a front rock (an accompanying rock placed in front of the master rock) is turned slightly forward it lends dignity to the master rock, which is well in view. The occasion on which a triangular rock is used for the master rock, however, does not come under this particular rule.

Figure 59   Figure 59 shows how to bury a rock. First, a hole must be dug twice as deep and wide as the volume of the rock to be used. Pebbles and mortar are placed on the bottom and well tamped. This forms a hard, compact foundation which is strong enough to support the rock and make it stable. After placing the rock on this foundation, more pebbles are used to fill in the gaps around the rock to keep it in a solid position. Then mortar is applied so that the rock will settle and become rooted in the ground.

Figures 60–63   When the rockwork has been selected, the whole area including the site of the rockwork placement is dug 3 feet 4 inches deep. Then the various sizes of rocks are rooted, following the plan of the garden construction. Generally a pulley and chains are used to carry and move the rocks. Upright rocks are positioned; flat rocks are laid at the proper spots or positions. The ridge of the master rock is then decided upon,

211

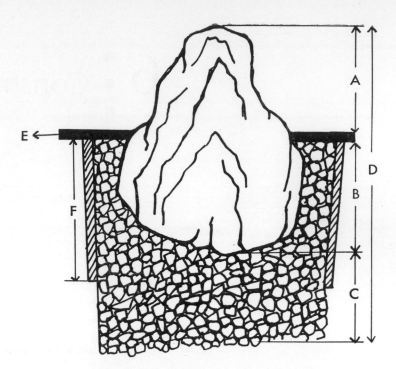

FIG. 59. Longitudinal section of a rock arrangement: A) exposed part; B) root (buried part);
C) bottom base of mortared and tamped pebbles;
D) distance between the top of the rock and its base
at the bottom; E) ground-cover, 2 to 4 inches thick,
or sand $1\frac{1}{4}$ inch thick on a 2-inch thickness of
earth; F) mortar enclosure, a thickness of 2 inches.

which requires selection of its front side. Next, accompanying rocks are
selected according to the ridge of the master rock, as they will be placed
at its left and right. The front rock is then arranged, followed by the
rear rock, which is placed in back of the master rock to add depth and
dimension to the composition. When the rocks are rooted in position,
earth is used to fill in to the level of the site before digging so that the
rocks look like natural stone outcrops. Lastly, fine gravel is spread to
a depth of $1\frac{1}{4}$ inches around the rocks as they emerge from the ground.
These pieces of gravel are usually just under $\frac{1}{4}$ inch in diameter and are
of crushed granite. They should be renewed once a year, as they are
affected by weathering.

The following remarks concern the overall appearance and maintenance of a stone garden. The wall surrounding the garden may be of
clay, bamboo fencing, or a natural hedge. Concrete walls and those
composed of blocks are to be avoided, as they destroy the harmonious
relationship between the garden and nature. White, dark yellow, and
brown colors are recommended for the wall. Essentially the garden has
no elements other than rocks. Weeds, however, will grow on the ground
or earthen part. Proper foundation work will prevent much of this, but
a certain amount of seed is inevitably blown in by the wind. Mortaring
of the ground surfaces retards seed germination, and only the space
assigned to moss as a ground cover should be left unmortared.

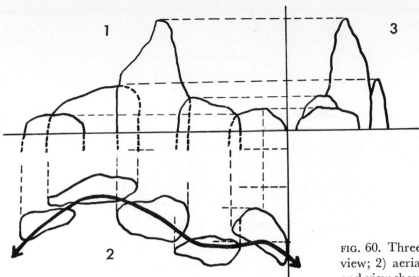

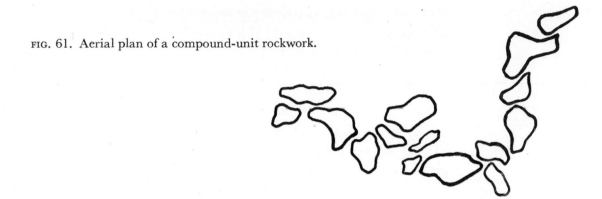

FIG. 60. Three views of a rockwork composition: 1) front view; 2) aerial view; 3) side view. The arrow of the second view shows the direction of the vigor of the ridge.

FIG. 61. Aerial plan of a compound-unit rockwork.

FIG. 62. Front view of the compound-unit rockwork. (Compare with Fig. 61)

FIG. 63. Component parts of a turtle island: 1) head stone; 2) limb stones; 3) tail stone. Young pine trees are usually planted on the turtle's back.

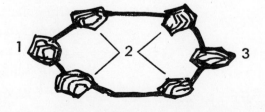

Spacing in a Stone Garden

Plates 185–202
Figures 64, 65

What is the ideal number and volume of rocks for use in a garden? Naturally it is impossible to give one answer because there are many conditions to consider, such as the location and topography of the garden site, its ultimate size, and the garden-maker's budget. The number and size of the stones will be determined when the conditions are completely understood and the plan designed.

The first consideration is the ratio between the garden area and the size and volume of the rockwork which is most appropriate for a stone garden. One large rock is equal in volume to from three to five medium rocks or from ten to twenty small rocks. Table 2 (p. 216) shows the ratio of the garden area to the rockwork size. Rocks are classified by size as follows: large is over two tons; medium, one to two tons, and small, one ton or less.

Figures (31, 32)

In the construction of rockwork, the average weight of rocks per 100 square feet is about 25 tons. Especially in *kazan* rockwork, rocks exceeding 25 tons are not ordinarily used. The garden plans of Ryoan-ji (Figs. 31, 32) are typical of an average garden showing that rockwork is used up to 10% of the total area. Thus the wider the space surrounding the rockwork the finer the aesthetic effect, and the better the balance and stability. The following is a translation of a quotation from *Tsukiyama-Teizo-den,* a text on landscaping published in 1735:

> Realize that it is most inharmonious to tower too many stones or rocks that are too large in a small garden or too small in a large garden. And it is also quite inharmonious if a small garden actually looks small.

To boast about the size or shape of rocks is not in keeping with the spirit and purpose of a Japanese stone garden, which is created as an attractive landscape to be enjoyed. Distinguished beauty is present in the Ryoan-ji garden because of its serene simplicity and skillful artistic effect. Regarding the use of rockwork to create mountain views, the same book states:

> To fold rocks [construct rockwork] is a means of creating the appearance of a mountain ravine in the garden. Combine them in compound units of three rocks. Handle supplementary and accompanying rocks with great care to compose mountain ranges in miniature, so that they look as though they were folded many times from the front to the rear. These are called "fold rocks." For example, the so-called thirteen or nineteen-folded rockwork does not mean that certain rocks are piled in thirteen or nineteen steps but that skillful treatment and composition of rocks makes the rockwork look thirteen or nineteen folded.

FIG. 64. "A Drawing of Scenic Rocks." This garden received its title from the 17th-century artist, Moronobu Hishikawa, who depicted it in ukiyo-e.

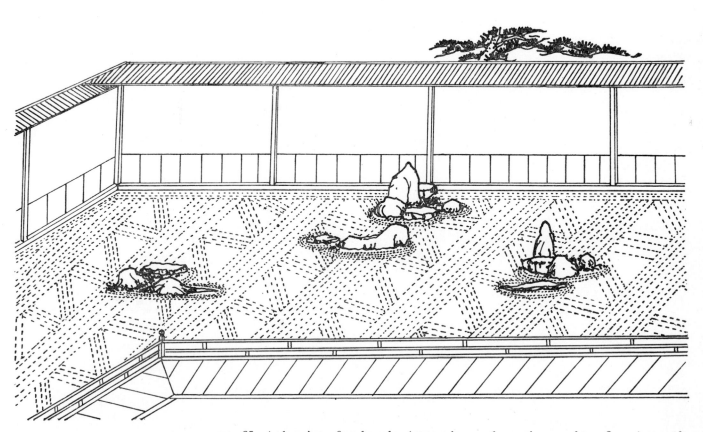

FIG. 65. A drawing of rockworks. A two-piece, a three-piece, and two five-piece rock-works are seen against the expanse of white sand.

The number of rocks required for a rockwork is also decided in terms of the garden's space. A garden cannot be regarded as splendid simply because it has numerous rocks; it is, however, highly appreciated when finely shaped rocks and rockwork of different sizes are used in skillful ratio providing visual variety. The ratio of spacing between the rockwork and the total garden area must first be considered. Design and style to fit the area are also of primary importance. In sum, a good stone garden is one which has fine spaces in relation to fine rock masses.

TABLE 2: RATIO OF ROCKWORK TO GARDEN AREA

Type of stone garden	Size of rock-work	Size and number of rocks			Ratio of rockwork to garden area	Total weight of rockwork in tons
		large	medium	small		
Kazan rockwork	large	2	5–6	8–10	90%	24–28
	small	1	3–4	5–6	70–80%	15½–19
Ordinary rockwork	large	1	2–3	3–4	50–60%	11–14
	medium	1	1–2	2–3	30–40%	6½–10
	small	0	1	4–5	1–5%	4½–6½

PLATE 185.　Miniature landscape of the Shimane Prefectural Office garden. Two three-piece rockworks stand in the enclosure of a white mortar garden path. These rockworks are distinguished for having good balance when seen from any direction. Each rockwork has a master rock and two accompanying rocks arranged following the ridge lines of the master rock. (Shimane Prefectural Office, Matsue, Shimane Pref.)

PLATE 186.   Large front yard of Daitsu-in. The huge rock expresses simplicity and sublimity. (Daitsu-in, Sokoku-ji, Kyoto)

PLATE 187. Miniature landscape garden composed mainly of scenic rocks. According to the garden's designer, the rock in the foreground and the two-piece rockwork in the rear are placed to simulate a noted mountain of Kiangsi Province, China. (Residential Stone Garden Exhibition held at Nijo Castle, Kyoto, *c.* 1965)

PLATE 188. Classical garden. The five Buddhist essentials (itsutsu-gusoku) are the theme of one of the basic garden compositions. Two upright rocks under the pine tree, a rectangular rock, white flat rock in front of the tree, and a horizontal rock in the foreground stand respectively for benevolence, justice, courtesy, intelligence, and confidence. (Residential Stone Garden Exhibit, Nijo Castle, Kyoto)

PLATE 189. Miniaturization of Ryoan-ji garden. This garden is a copy of Ryoan-ji in one-seventh the area (646 square feet). It comprises rockwork in four groupings, from left to right, of one, two, three, and two pieces mounted on moss. The sensitivity to proportion and the unified quality of the material make vivid the entire composition centering around the master rockwork. (Araki residence, Kyoto)

PLATE 190. Front view. The vigor of the rocks is well expressed in this garden. (Araki residence, Kyoto)

PLATE 191 *(facing page)*. Side view. The material used is diorite proper, a hard mountain rock. (Araki residence, Kyoto)

PLATE 192.   Scenic rockwork. The handling of the front accompanying stone with its forward slant demonstrates the basic form of a classical rockwork. Both this supplementary rock and the one at the rear are placed in an extended line from the ridge of the master rock. Sphagnum grows over the master rock in patches resembling blossoms. (Komyo Zen-in, Tofuku-ji, Kyoto)

222

PLATE 193.   Classical garden centering on mittsu-gusoku. The rocks are arranged with consideration for what they represent as well as for their size and shape. From left to right are the deity rock, worship rock (rock of heaven), immovable rock (rock of earth), and peaceful life rock (rock of man). Two deity rocks are in the right foreground; the three rocks in the left rear are sanzon-seki, and the two rocks at the foot of the hill in the right background are kei-seki. The rocks representing heaven, earth, and man symbolize the three essentials of Buddhism (mittsu-gusoku) found in classical ikebana. This garden thus represents a vast Buddhist universe with fetish rocks. However, leaving aside its iconographic meaning, the garden can be appreciated for the abstract beauty of the stones. The pavement of flagstone in a mosaic pattern shows a contemporary use of material. (Imai residence, Kyoto)

PLATE 194. Worship stone, or rock of heaven. (Imai residence, Kyoto)

PLATE 195. Immovable rock, or rock of earth. The master rock is in the shape of a tortoise, representing the protection of the house. (Imai residence, Kyoto)

PLATE 196.   Coastal view in miniature. Rocks on the mossy hillock at right depict mountain ranges; black stones represent the seashore at Wakasa Bay, and white sand the sea. This is a good example of realistic representation in garden-making. The garden's area is 355 square feet. (Residential Stone Garden Exhibition, Nijo Castle, Kyoto)

PLATE 197.   Detail of the garden. (Residential Stone Garden Exhibition, Nijo Castle, Kyoto)

PLATE 198.   Typical miniature landscape garden. A Buddhist pagoda towers in the center of the hill at left. Water represented by white sand spills down from the dry waterfall on the right and flows under the stone bridge *(far left)*. Twenty-two pieces of mountain rock (andesite) are used for the rockwork. The plants surrounding the garden are Japanese and Chinese black pine, Japanese maple, Ternstroemia japonica (mokoku), Japanese cedar, azalea, and hair moss. They give variety of color to the composition. The garden has an area of 355 square feet. (Residential Stone Garden Show, Nijo Castle, Kyoto)

PLATE 199.   Full view of garden and pagoda. (Stone Garden Show, Nijo Castle, Kyoto)

PLATE 200. Karataki at Saimyo-ji. The large rock on the left is the waterfall rock. Water appears to run down over a step, and white pebbles below simulate the fall's swirling movement. (Saimyo-ji, Shiga Pref.)

PLATE 201. Another karataki at Saimyo-ji. The master rock at left has a concave surface. (Saimyo-ji, Shiga Pref.)

PLATE 202.　Full view of the karataki rockwork. This magnificent dry waterfall rockwork has five levels and is the largest karataki in Japan (6 feet 8 inches tall). The rock at the top has the typical three-piece composition. All of sixteen stones used in this rockwork are of rhyolite, the grain of which well simulates running water. (Ryotan-ji, Hikone, Shiga Pref.)

228

7 : Garden Paths

THERE IS no path in a garden constructed purely to be viewed. However, one is necessary in a garden which is to be walked in and to lead a guest from the front gate to the entrance of a garden or through its various parts. The path may be composed of steppingstones, loosely inlaid stone pavement *(nobedan)*, compactly inlaid stone pavement *(shiki-ishi)*, marsh steppingstones *(sawa-watari)*, stone bridges, or foot stones. All of these elements are quite unique in their utility and beauty.

Steppingstones

Plates 203–222   Steppingstones for a garden path should be carefully selected for their shape, utility, and environmental harmony. The garden-maker must first consider their practical use as material for a walk. Then he should see that they contribute aesthetically to the composition of the garden. Both natural and cut stones are used for steppingstones; granite is usually the material used for cut stones.

One must consider the factors of accessibility and convenience in placing steppingstones. Places with heavy traffic to and from a house are not good for such a path. Thus steppingstones are constructed only within the garden itself or used to form a path to the garden entrance. The distance of a person's step is one of the most important considerations in arranging steppingstones. The average man walks 119 steps a minute on level ground, and his average step is 25 inches. The average woman walks 124 steps a minute; her average step is just under 19 inches. Thus the distance between two steppingstones should be from 8 to 12 inches, or slightly shorter than the average length of a step. The steppingstone varies in size from one which will accommodate the width of a single foot to a stone which will accommodate both feet. A one-foot stone is smaller than 16 inches on a side, while a two-foot stone is larger than 16 inches on each side.

There are some stones which are naturally more suitable for steppingstones than others in quality, size, and shape. The stone must be hard, so sandstone and tuff are to be avoided. Andesite mountain rock is regarded as best for this use. Stones with a plane surface must be

229

selected; concave stones should not be used because rain water would stand in the depressions, making them unfit for walking. Stones with a naturally smooth surface are preferred, but ones which have been leveled by artificial means are also used. Regarding shape, the pentagonal and hexagonal ones (which include the turtle-shaped stone) are considered best.

Although steppingstones usually have to be the same quality of stone, sometimes different types of stone or cut stones are mixed in with the others. These affect the tone and pattern of the steppingstones and thus the feelings of the person walking on them. In Japan architectural foundation stones and millstones are often used in this manner. Sometimes roofing tiles, bricks, or ceramic pieces are used. It is important to realize that such materials should be used with great restraint, and a ratio of 10% of these to the main stone material is about the maximum allowable in path construction. Although unusual stones give variety to a steppingstone path, the quality of refinement would be lost if the ratio were higher.

Figure 66   In Japanese the verb used to describe arranging steppingstones is "to strike" them. This better expresses their vigor and is more suggestive of the handling given them than the words "set" or "place." The linear element is indispensable in a path of steppingstones because it determines the direction the stones will take. The line they will follow is designed first. After this, two parallel ropes or cords 8 inches apart are laid according to the plan for the path. These cords are set at a height of 4 inches from the ground to act as a standard for the height of the stones. The rooting or burying of the stones is fairly shallow, only one-third the thickness of the stone. The stones are set on a well-tamped earthen base or on a stable foundation of inlaid gravel, if the ground tends to be soft. The order of striking the stones is as follows, as shown in Figure 66: the first stone is placed at the starting position of the path; the second stone at the end position; the third stone is placed midway between them or at the branching position, if a path branches off to the side; the fourth stone is set midway between the second and the third stones, and thus each stone is arranged between the two previously struck stones.

Regarding the linking of steppingstones, every stone has a head and hips; when stones are connected to form steppingstones, the hips of the first stone must meet the head of the second stone. These are linked visually by the vigor of the stones, as in the case of rockwork arrangements previously described. Three stones of the same size and shape are not placed in a line together; they are arranged slightly off line. When a one-foot stone is repeated twice, the third must be a two-foot stone.

Figure 67   A steppingstone path is composed of a combination of double-stone and triple-stone units. There is great variation in the combination of large (two-foot) and small (one-foot) stones:

1. *Two-three strike*. The combinations of a double-stone unit plus a triple-stone unit are: one large and one small rock plus two large and one small; one small and one large plus two small and one large; two large plus two small and one large, or two small plus two large and one small, etc.

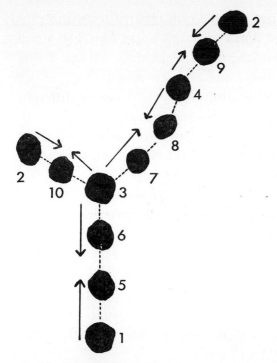

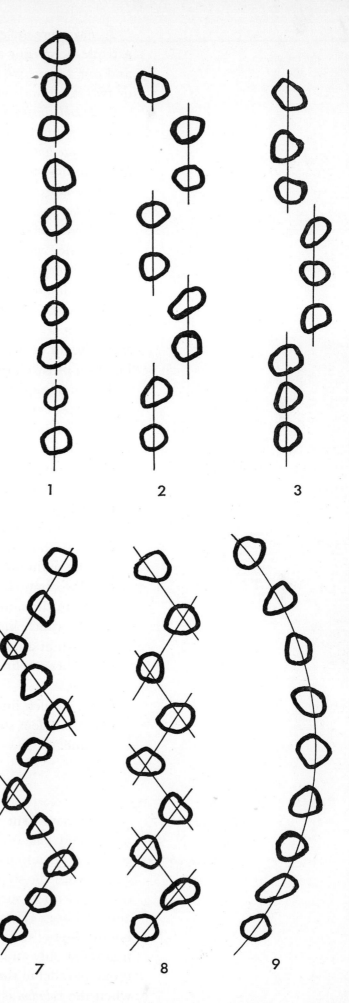

FIG. 66. Steppingstones forming a garden path. Basic rocks are: 1) starting stone; 2) terminal stones; 3) branching-off stone. The numbers indicate the order of rock placement, and the arrows direct the order of the strikes.

1

2

3

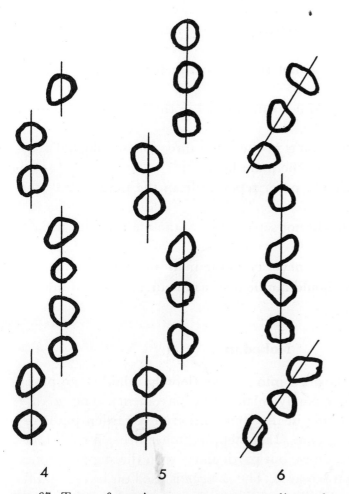

4

5

6

7

8

9

FIG. 67. Types of steppingstone arrangements: 1) two-three strike; 2) variation of double-linked strike; 3) variation of triple-linked strike; 4) variation of two-four strike; 5) variation of two-three strike; 6) variation of three-four strike; 7) wild-goose strike; 8) plover strike; 9) grand-curve strike.

2. *Four-three strike*. The combinations of a quaternary-stone unit plus a triple-stone unit are: two large and two small rocks plus two small and one large; two small and two large plus two small and one large, or two large and two small plus two large and one small, etc.

3. *Double-linked strike*. The combinations of two stones of different sizes, large and small, the same units of distance apart.

4. *Triple-linked strike*. The combinations of two stones of similar size and another stone different in size, a large and two small, or a small and two large, the same units of distance apart.

5. *Wild-goose strike*. Stones combined to simulate wild geese in flight.

6. *Plover strike*. Stones combined to simulate the marks a plover makes when walking on the ground.

7. *Grand-curve strike*. Steppingstones laid in a curve. There are various combinations of the above in which rocks are placed according to size and curve. The preferable distance between two adjacent stones is 8 to 10 inches. This length is the standard for the combinations of two small stones or a large and a small stone. The standard for the combination of two large stones is 10 to 12 inches.

The steppingstone line often branches in some other direction, which necessitates construction of a path or paths leading off from the main one. The following should be observed in the construction of these branch lines:

(1) A branch line should not stem from the inside curve of the main line of the path.

(2) A branch line should not run parallel in the same direction as the main line.

(3) A branch line should not run parallel in the reverse direction of the main line.

(4) Two branch lines going in the same direction should not start from the same side of the main line.

(5) A branch line should never separate from the main line of the path at an acute angle.

(6) A branch line should not separate from the main line at a right angle.

(7) A branch line should never cross the main line at right angles.

(8) A one-foot stone should not be used as the first stone of a branch line.

Nobedan

Plates (213, 217, 218), 223–236
Figures 68, 69

Stone pavement is classified into *nobedan* (loosely inlaid stone pavement) and *shiki-ishi* (compactly inlaid stone pavement). The *nobedan* performs an important role in the composition of a garden path, together with the steppingstones. Like steppingstones it has a close relationship with its surroundings, but particularly with the steppingstones and buildings of the garden area. The *nobedan* is used on level ground, not on sloping surfaces. Unlike steppingstones it is given straight, linear treatment only and is never curved. The most desirable line for *nobedan* is one parallel to the building near it. There is one exception, however, when the *nobedan* is obliged to curve somewhat because of the structure

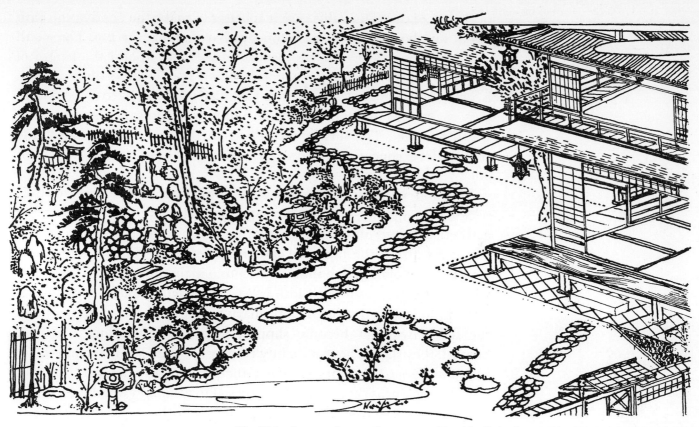

FIG. 68. Nobedan and steppingstones. Double-linked steppingstones curve at an obtuse angle and meet the main line of the nobedan. The large foundation stone of a building is used at the junction.

FIG. 69. Garden paths. Shown here are nobedan used for the main line and stepping-stones for the branch lines. The former gives the straight-line element; the latter, that of a dotted curve.

of the site, but even in this case it is better to make the bend in the path out of supplementary steppingstones rather than use *nobedan*. The width of the pavement depends on the size of the garden and the length of the path, but a very wide pavement is not used. The ordinary width is between $2\frac{1}{2}$ and 3 feet, which is sufficient to allow two people to pass each other on the walk. The minimum allowance should be a width of 2 feet. The surface of the pavement must be level or slightly convex, for a concave surface would collect and hold water after a rainfall.

The materials used to compose a *nobedan* cannot be too carefully selected. Flagstones of irregular shape and size are used to create an aesthetically interesting effect. A path with an irregular appearing surface is the aim of the Japanese garden-maker when constructing a *nobedan*. The size of flagstone should be $3\frac{1}{2}$ to 6 inches if the *nobedan* is 2 feet wide; $4\frac{1}{2}$ to 7 inches if the width is 2 feet $7\frac{1}{4}$ inches, and 7 to $8\frac{1}{4}$ inches if the path is a yard wide. The primary prerequisite in selection is that the stones will not become slippery with dampness and moisture. Second, they should have a slightly convex surface. A third requirement is that all stones be of approximately the same quality; a hard substance must be chosen, as these stones are exposed to wear and weather. Natural shapes are preferable, but cut stones may also be used. The types of stone used are andesite and granite. Stones in moderate sizes without artificial touches are most commonly selected for *nobedan;* an example is the two-pyroxene andesite rock. Sandstone and tuff wear too easily and so are not used.

Figures 70, 71   The steps in constructing a *nobedan* are given below:

1. *Digging the bed.* The foundation for the bed is made the same way that rockwork is rooted; that is, the area is dug 4 inches deep. (This soil may be disposed of because it is not used later in any part of the construction.)

2. *Laying the bed.* Small cracked stones or pebbles are placed on the bottom of the bed and tamped with a pressure hammer. Clay may be used to lay the bed, but concrete is not used in place of the stones or clay.

3. *Paneling.* Two pieces of board 8 inches high are braced on edge at either side of the bed. The stones will be laid within these forms. The main purpose of the framing is to keep the long sides of the *nobedan* straight (Figs. 70, 71). Accordingly, the stones which are laid in the bed must have one straight side which is placed against the wood of the frame. Corner stones must be set at right angles and should have two straight sides.

4. *Roping.* Two ropes or lengths of cord are set lengthwise on either side of the form of the *nobedan* about 2 to 4 inches high to keep the stones at a level height. (This leveling line is the same kind used in the laying of steppingstones or brick and is set at the proper height for the *nobedan*.)

5. *Inlaying with stones.* The long sides of the *nobedan* section of the path are first composed, then the two short ends. When this framework is completed the wooden board framing is removed. To fill in the center area, if the material is to be mixed, other stones such as millstones or

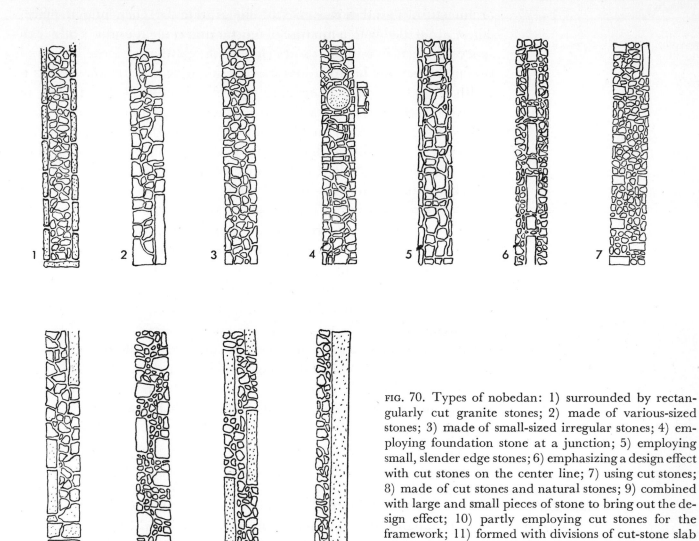

FIG. 70. Types of nobedan: 1) surrounded by rectangularly cut granite stones; 2) made of various-sized stones; 3) made of small-sized irregular stones; 4) employing foundation stone at a junction; 5) employing small, slender edge stones; 6) emphasizing a design effect with cut stones on the center line; 7) using cut stones; 8) made of cut stones and natural stones; 9) combined with large and small pieces of stone to bring out the design effect; 10) partly employing cut stones for the framework; 11) formed with divisions of cut-stone slab and natural stone composition.

FIG. 71. Corner stones. Every corner stone must have a right angle. (The only exception occurs when the nobedan curves at an obtuse angle.) Corner stones as well as all framing stones must be about 4 inches thick because they protect the frame edges and are viewed from the sides.

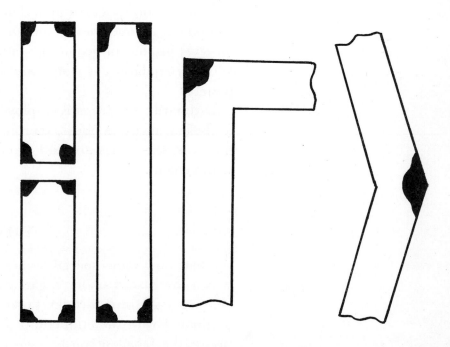

architectural foundation stones of cut granite are then put in place. These are settled with a mixture of mortar and cement underneath. The space between two inlaid stones should be less than $\frac{1}{2}$ inch. Gaps between the various inlaid stones may be made with a trowel having a width of under $\frac{1}{2}$ inch. These gaps are very effective in the creation of an interesting pattern. They should not cross one another—the lines are formed in a "T", not in an "X" shape. Also, long straight lines should be avoided; only if flagstones of various types are used will the lines of the path have the desired appearance of intricacy. The depth of the gaps between the stones is about $\frac{3}{4}$ inch.

6. *Mortaring the gaps*. The stones are joined at the base with white mortar. (If another color is desired, for example gray, it may be made by mixing powdered dye with the mortar until the desired color is obtained. Any color of dye powder may be mixed with the mortar depending on personal preference; earthen tones, however, are preferable.) It is left to nature to cover the mortar with accumulated dirt or a growth of moss.

Different effects can be achieved by mixing cut stones of various shapes. Schistose stones in varied colors may be used in addition to two-pyroxene andesite. Some of these are chlorite schist, epidote schist, anthopyllite schist, actinolite schist, and amphibole schist.

Shiki-ishi

Plates 237–246
Figure 72

A compactly inlaid stone pavement is called *shiki-ishi*. It is found not only in Japan but in Western countries as well, where it is used for gardens, parks, and street pavings. The Japanese handling of stones and design, however, shows evidence of the country's unique traditions, for the treatment of cut stones and their expression of beauty and utility are not found in Western style pavements.

Shiki-ishi are also called "cut-stone pavements" in Japan because they contain uniformly cut stones. These may be square, rectangular, triangular, trapezoid, hexagonal, or irregular in shape. They are inlaid on level ground in geometric patterns, such as checks and hexagons. When irregularly cut stones are employed, the gaps form a cracked pattern.

Ordinarily a *shiki-ishi* is employed to form a path from an outer gate to the entrance of a house. Its construction is similar to that of *nobedan;* however, the stones are laid as close together as possible and joined with cement.

Yaku-ishi

Plates 247–253
Figure 73

There are some special stones called functional stones *(yaku-ishi)* which are placed under a gate as foot stones. These have a definite character and are used in Japanese homes and teahouses. *Yaku-ishi* originated with the etiquette of the tea ceremony; their use well expresses the Japanese spirit.

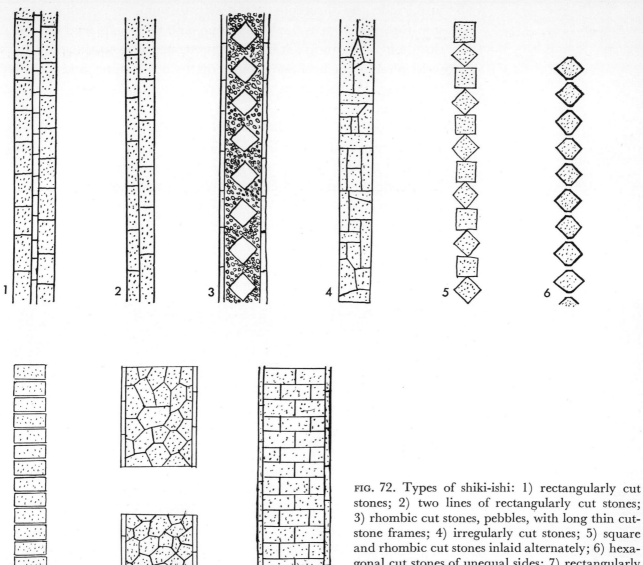

FIG. 72. Types of shiki-ishi: 1) rectangularly cut stones; 2) two lines of rectangularly cut stones; 3) rhombic cut stones, pebbles, with long thin cut-stone frames; 4) irregularly cut stones; 5) square and rhombic cut stones inlaid alternately; 6) hexagonal cut stones of unequal sides; 7) rectangularly cut stones in line; 8) cut stones forming a cracked pattern; 9) a regular pattern of rectangularly cut stones.

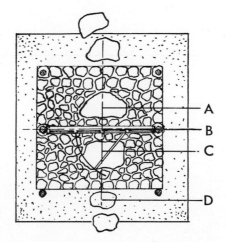

FIG. 73. Yaku-ishi. A) guest's stone; B) threshold; C) step-through stone; D) host's stone. The functional stones, except for the host's stone, are surrounded by a nobedan pavement. (Omote Senke school of tea, Kyoto)

Functional stones are placed on either side of the threshold. The stone just inside the threshold is the step-through stone; that nearest the step-through stone is the host's stone, and the one placed outside of the threshold is the guest's stone. The guest, standing on the guest's stone, is welcomed by the host, who stands on the host's stone, and is invited into the house. He then steps through onto the inside stones, thus entering the house.

The host's stone is placed lower than the guest and step-through stones, and the distance between host and guest is about 40 inches. As seen in Figure 73, the host's stone is placed outside of the pavement. The stone placements themselves compel the host and guest to extend courtesies to each other. When the host meets his guest at the gate he receives him modestly, and they exchange bows. When he sees him off at the gate he shows his respect by bowing again. Thus the placement of stones at a threshold involves an understanding of Japanese etiquette. The actual laying of these stones is done in the same manner as for the *nobedan.*

COLOR PLATE 4 *(facing page).* Raikyu-ji, Takahashi, Okayama Pref.

MAKING A STONE GARDEN 238

PLATE 203. Path to the teahouse of the Sakaguchi residence. The line is that of a simple, functional path starting from the bamboo gates. It divides into three branches: to the stone water basin on the right, to the entrance of the teahouse, and to the far side of the teahouse. Both diverging points have two-foot stones. This design makes use of the contrast between the straight line of the nobedan and the curves of the steppingstones. (Sakaguchi residence, Kyoto)

PLATE 204.   The material used here is granite cut and arranged like a compactly inlaid stone pavement. Artificial touches within each slab give variety to the composition, relieving the monotony of the repeated rectangular form. (Residential Stone Garden Show, Nijo Castle, Kyoto)

PLATE 205.   Steppingstone stairway. This is one of the few examples of steppingstones used for a stairway. The stones are two-foot ones placed horizontally. (Katsura residence, Kyoto)

PLATE 206.   Steppingstone arrangement. Every concave edge meets a convex one in this harmonious arrangement. When the distance between stones is too far to step, a small attendant stone (hikae-ishi) is inserted between the two (e.g., the second stone from the front, which is placed slightly lower than the other stones). (Katsura residence, Kyoto)

PLATE 207. Steppingstones with attendant stones. The standard size of attendant stones is one foot. The smaller stone in the foreground and the one by the branching-off stone are both hikae-ishi. (Ura Senke school of tea, Kyoto)

PLATE 208. Two-three strike steppingstone path. Two one-foot stones and one two-foot stone form one unit and two onefoot stones form the other unit. (Katsura residence, Kyoto)

PLATE 209. Steppingstones of a triple-linked strike with attendant stones. Every third stone is a two-foot stone; the small stones on the left-hand side are all attendant stones and are not counted in the number of steppingstones. (Shoren-in, Kyoto)

PLATE 210. Triple-linked strike. The pattern consists of two small stones followed by a two-foot stone. Linking the head and hips of the stones gives them life and vigor. (Katsura residence, Kyoto)

PLATE 211. Steppingstones with a lookout stone. The steppingstones are composed of two-three strikes. In the foreground is the large, flat lookout stone (monomi-ishi) on which one stops to view and enjoy the garden. (Katsura residence, Kyoto)

PLATE 212. Two-foot steppingstones. These stones are scrupulously arranged with consideration for their utility as well as the aesthetic effect of the curving design. Attendant stones are placed at the corners of the curves. (Shugaku-in, Kyoto)

PLATE 213. Intersecting steppingstones and nobedan. A lookout rock is placed by the steppingstones where they intersect with the nobedan so that the garden viewer may stop to enjoy the scenery. (Katsura residence, Kyoto)

PLATE 214. Even steppingstones of a two-three strike. The apparently straight line of the steppingstones emits vigor through the good linking of head and hips. (Katsura residence, Kyoto)

PLATE 215.   Steppingstones below a veranda. At the pentagonal branching-off stone, two different types of steppingstone paths diverge, leading toward the nobedan. (Katsura residence, Kyoto)

PLATE 216.   Detail of the steppingstone stairs. Every stone of the stairs is placed with attention to comfortable step distance, one of the most important considerations in making a steppingstone path. (Katsura residence, Kyoto)

248

PLATE 217. Steppingstones and nobedan at Seison-kaku. A combination of elements make this an interesting path. The viewer's attention progresses from the rectangularly cut flagstone to the two round, flat steppingstones, and finally to the nobedan. (Seison-kaku, Kanazawa, Ishikawa Pref.)

PLATE 218. Steppingstones and nobedan. Beauty of form is emphasized here. (Koho-an, Kyoto)

249

PLATE 219. Steppingstones with a mill-stone. (Raikyu-ji, Takahashi, Okayama Pref.)

PLATE 220. Steppingstones of a two-three strike. The distance between the stepping-stones is quite short, indicating that the garden-maker wants the viewer to walk at a leisurely pace in order to enjoy every aspect of the garden. (Shoren-in, Kyoto)

250

PLATE 221. Steppingstones of a triple-linked strike. (Koho-an, Kyoto)

PLATE 222. Steppingstones of a plover strike. Two-foot, one-foot, and smaller stones are arranged in a zigzag pattern. (Koho-an, Kyoto)

PLATE 224.   Nobedan of chlorite schist. This magnificent nobedan composed with stones of various sizes has a carefully manipulated framing. It was built about three hundred years ago and is 65 feet 6 inches long, 3 feet 4 inches wide, and 4 inches thick. The material used to fill the gaps between the stones is clay mixed with powdered limestone. (Ikkyu-ji, Kyoto)

PLATE 223 *(facing page)*.   Nobedan framed with large flagstones. The stones inlaid inside the frame are waste rock materials, combining with the flagstones to create an effective composition. (Katsura residence, Kyoto)

PLATE 225. Nobedan of large and small stones. This nobedan with its framing of large stones is composed in a manner similar to that of Plate 224. (Katsura residence, Kyoto)

PLATE 226. Nobedan crossed with steppingstones. Although the design of this path looks very modern it is three hundred and fifty years old; its novel design will always attract the eye of the garden viewer. The nobedan of schistose rocks is constructed around the square-cut granite steppingstones. (Katsura residence, Kyoto)

254

PLATE 227. Typical nobedan. Made of two-pyroxene andesite, the path has a beautiful irregular pattern composed of stones of various sizes. The zigzag lines of the gaps are achieved by a combination of small split rock pieces and add interesting movement to the design, emphasizing natural rather than artificial beauty. This kind of expression through use of material is typically Japanese, representing the traditional blending of utility with beauty. (Rokuo-in, Kyoto)

PLATE 228. Detail of nobedan. The composition of the stones shows clearly here. (Rokuo-in, Kyoto)

255

PLATE 229. Cut-stone nobedan. Large cut flagstones of chlorite schist are inlaid following the center line of the path, and small split stones fill the spaces between the central part and the granite stones of the framing. This 17th-century nobedan has good contrast of color, for the green of the large stone slabs shows well against the white of the framing rocks. This gorgeous and costly nobedan contains more than fifty schistose slabs and is 98 feet 6 inches long and just under 4 feet wide. (Kaizando, Tofuku-ji, Kyoto)

PLATE 230. Detail of nobedan stones. (Kaizando, Tofuku-ji, Kyoto)

256

PLATE 231. Schistose nobedan. Mostly schistose rocks are used; but two large, natural granite stones are inlaid, one at each end. (Jiko-in, Nara Pref.)

PLATE 232. Cut-flagstone nobedan. This pavement is composed of cut granite slabs, round medium-sized rocks, and stones. (Ura Senke school of tea, Kyoto)

PLATE 233. Nobedan with foundation stone. This path is composed mainly of split stones, with a large foundation stone approximately halfway to vary what would otherwise be a monotonous pattern. (Nishimura residence, Kyoto)

PLATE 234. Nobedan and shiki-ishi. (Joan-no-seki, Kanagawa Pref.)

PLATE 235. Nobedan of roofing tiles. This novel use of tiles has a refreshing quality and seems quite modern. (Kanden-an, Matsue, Shimane Pref.)

PLATE 236. Nobedan including a cut flagstone. A large, square schistose stone links with the three rows of split stones to create a novel pavement. The gaps around the stones particularly catch the viewer's eye. (Joan-no-seki, Kanagawa Pref.)

PLATE 237.   Cracked stone shiki-ishi. Stones are compactly inlaid to form the pavement of a road. (Katsura residence, Kyoto)

PLATE 238.   Brick-patterned shiki-ishi of cut stones. (Joanno-seki, Kanagawa Pref.)

PLATE 239. Shiki-ishi combined with nobedan. The nobedan is the pavement at right extending to the rear. (Omote Senke school of tea, Kyoto)

PLATE 240. Cut-stone shiki-ishi in a cracked pattern. (Omote Senke school of tea, Kyoto)

PLATE 241. Shiki-ishi of evenly cut stones.
Natural stones border it on either side.
(Rokuo-in, Kyoto)

PLATE 242. Shiki-ishi of square-cut stones.
The stones are set in a diamond pattern along
the center line of the path. (Mampuku-ji, Uji,
Kyoto Pref.)

PLATE 243.   Cracked-stone shiki-ishi laid like nobedan. (Joan-no-seki, Kanagawa Pref.)

PLATE 244.   Cut-stone shiki-ishi of one rectangular slab. (Nishimura residence, Kyoto)

PLATE 245. Shiki-ishi with a triplet-row pattern of obliquely inlaid square-cut stones. (Nishimura residence, Kyoto)

PLATE 246. Winding cracked-stone shiki-ishi. The stones are arranged to look like nobedan. (Nishimura residence, Kyoto)

PLATE 247. Two functional stones. In the foreground is the step-through stone, and behind it is the guest's stone. A cracked-stone pavement surrounds them. (Omote Senke school of tea, Kyoto)

PLATE 248. Functional stones and path. These functional stones are incorporated into the design of the path: the guest stone is set in the path while the step-through stone on the inside of the threshold is placed as the extension of the path. (Ura Senke school of tea, Kyoto)

266

PLATES 249–251. Functional stones. Plate 249 *(facing page, above)* shows the guest's stone set in a pavement of cracked stones with the step-through stone just visible beyond the threshold. The host's stone *(above)* is the separately placed square one in the foreground. A cut-stone shiki-ishi *(facing page, below)* completes the path from the functional stones to the house entrance. (Katsura, residence, Kyoto)

267

PLATE 252. Typical placement of functional stones. The guest's stone is placed on the far side of the threshold and is higher than the step-through and host's stones. Only the host's stone is arranged amid the covering of pine needles. (Joan-no-seki, Kanagawa Pref.)

PLATE 253. Simplified functional stones. In the front are the guest's stone and stone threshold, behind which are the step-through and host's stones. (Joan-no-seki, Kanagawa Pref.)

PLATE 254.   Linear and circular sand patterns. Surrounding the rocks are ripples and water rings to depict a sea. (Ryoan-ji, Kyoto)

PLATE 255.   Sand raking. A whirlpool pattern is raked from the central point to the outer rim of the circle.

PLATE 256.   Sand rake. A wooden rake with a saw-toothed edge is used to create patterns.

270

PLATE 257. Water-ring patterns. The sand at right is raked into water rings. A sand pile is seen at the left. (Ryozoku-in, Kennin-ji, Kyoto)

PLATE 258.   Sand piles. This garden composed entirely of white sand is decorated with two sand piles. On ceremonial occasions they are flattened. The running-water pattern is employed here. (Daisen-in, Daitoku-ji, Kyoto)

PLATE 259.   Running-water pattern. (Tenju-an, Nanzen-ji, Kyoto)

PLATE 260.   Ripplets and running-water patterns. This garden composed entirely of white, orange, and brown sand is located in the yard of the Nikka whisky factory. The three colors represent the crude liquors. (Nikka whisky factory, Nishinomiya, Hyogo Pref.)

273

PLATES 261–264. Sand dais. The patterns are described with a wooden board by one of the monks of the temple. Creating sand patterns is part of a monk's religious training; a new design is made each day, since yesterday's creation cannot be today's study. Plates depict *(facing page)* two flowers and water; *(top to bottom)* a chrysanthemum floating in water; on the right two maple leaves and running water on the left; a single flower on the right and a paulownia leaf on the left. (Honen-in, Kyoto)

PLATE 265.   Sand dais symbolizing a lake. This design originated in the 18th century.
The sand pattern is of ripplets. (Ginkaku-ji, Kyoto)

276

PLATE 266.   Whirlpool patterns. (Tofuku-ji, Kyoto)

PLATE 267.   Swirling-water pattern. (Shimane Prefectural
Office, Matsue, Shimane Pref.)

PLATE 268 (*facing page*). Checkered pattern. This design symbolizes rice fields. Vertical and horizontal patterns are raked, leaving alternate spaces blank. (Kaizando, Tofuku-ji, Kyoto)

PLATE 269. Moss garden. More than twenty varieties besides hair moss grow wild in this temple garden. Here the moisture of the earth is especially suited for the growth of mosses, and a foggy climate stimulates growth. (Saiho-ji, Kyoto)

PLATES 273 and 274. Moss hillocks. These well-developed hair-moss hillocks resemble a luxuriant and beautiful green carpet. The moss of this garden has grown continually for over seventy years. (Sampo-in, Daikaku-ji, Kyoto)

PLATE 275. Rock arrangement with a water basin in the middle (naka-bachi tsukubai). In this arrangement a stone lantern replaces the candle-stand stone. (Residential Stone Garden Show, Nijo Castle, Kyoto)

PLATE 276. Natural stone naka-bachi tsukubai. (Sakaguchi residence, Kyoto)

PLATE 277. Natural stone naka-bachi tsukubai amid pebbles. Other functional stones are seen behind the narcissus in the foreground. (Sakaguchi residence, Kyoto)

PLATE 278. Corner naka-bachi tsukubai. The water pipe (kakehi) is made of bamboo. (Stone Garden Exhibition, held at Matsuya department store, Tokyo, in 1965)

PLATE 279. Rock arrangement with a tsukubai at the edge (muko-bachi tsukubai). This water basin has reliefs of Buddhist images on the four sides. (Stone Garden Show, Matsuya department store, Tokyo)

PLATE 280. Naka-bachi tsukubai. This is simply composed with a naturally hollowed basin and a foot stone. (Stone Garden Show, Matsuya department store, Tokyo)

PLATE 281. Rounded naka-bachi tsukubai. A stone lantern in the background replaces the candle-stand stone. (Residential Stone Garden Show, Nijo Castle, Kyoto)

PLATE 282. Rectangular tsukubai. The water basin is placed on the stone stand, and a ladle is set to one side. (Ginkaku-ji, Kyoto)

PLATE 283. Tsukubai placed by a pond. The large foot stone in front is arranged to form part of the bank. (Katsura residence, Kyoto)

PLATE 284.   Round tsukubai. (Katsura residence, Kyoto)

PLATE 285.   Rectangular tsukubai. The rectangular foot stone
links the basin with the steppingstones. (Katsura residence, Kyoto)

PLATE 286. Ornamented tsukubai. This water basin placed by the end of a veranda has four owls carved in relief. (Manju-in, Kyoto)

PLATE 287. Decorative tsukubai. This basin is for appreciation rather than use. (Kanso-an, Naritasan Betsu-in, Neyagawa, Osaka Pref.)

PLATE 288.   Oribe lantern. This 17th-century lantern has a Buddhist
image carved on its base. (Shugaku-in, Kyoto)

290

PLATE 289. Shade-roofed lanterns. (Renge-ji, Kyoto)

PLATE 290. Snow-viewing lantern with crescent-moon hollow. The lantern is placed so that one may view the garden on a snowy night. (Shugaku-in, Kyoto)

PLATE 291. Low lantern. (Katsura residence, Kyoto)

PLATE 292. Kimono-sleeve lantern. This ornamental lantern is named for its resemblance to the squared sleeve of the kimono. (Shugaku-in, Kyoto)

292

PLATE 293.　Double-window snow-viewing lantern. (Katsura residence, Kyoto)

PLATE 294.　Kotoji lantern. The kotoji is the bridge of the traditional Japanese harp (koto). This practical and decorative lantern has posts in the kotoji shape. (Kenroku Park, Kanazawa, Ishikawa Pref.)

PLATES 295–297. Garden with stone lantern. The slender stone lantern is attractive in this small garden (323 square feet). Placed in a corner of the garden area, it harmonizes with the entire scenic unit and exemplifies the skillful placement of a stone accessory. (Residential Stone Garden Show, Nijo Castle, Kyoto)

PLATE 298. Aerial view of winding stream and surrounding dais. Six guests are the maximum number that can sit on the dais beside the snaking stream. A faucet concealed behind the rocks in the left corner controls the stream's flow. (Suntory Brewery, Kawasaki, Kanagawa Pref.)

PLATE 299. Detail of the winding stream. The water flows from the left waterway and moves in a zigzag pattern before returning via the waterway at the right. (Suntory Brewery, Kawasaki, Kanagawa Pref.)

8 : Completing the Garden

Sand Patterns

Plates 254–268

Figure 74

In addition to rocks, sand or gravel is an indispensable material for a stone garden. Usually gravel made from crushed granite is used; fine sand from beaches, mountains, and rivers is not suitable for the stone garden. As we have seen in the classical gardens presented here, there are various patterns which may be described on the sand. These have been used since the 17th century and are symbolic designs representing the flow of water. The size of the grains used varies according to what is being depicted. For example, coarse gravel ($\frac{1}{2}$ inch in diameter) is used to express a rapid current or a waterfall; when a large rockwork is included in the garden area, this type is also used. On the other hand, a finer gravel (grains $\frac{1}{4}$ inch in diameter) is used in smaller garden areas.

A wooden rake is necessary to make the patterns (Plate 255). If one wishes to draw broad lines, a rake having edges with an obtuse angle is used; a rake the edges of which are at an acute angle is used for finer patterns. The sand patterns must be re-created daily because they are broken and disrupted by wind and rain. Also the sand should be replaced once a year because it becomes weathered and discolored. White sand of finely grained marble or quartz should never be used for stone gardens because the luster would spoil the quality of refinement of the garden as a whole. Such sand is only used for window displays or *bonseki* (stones in a miniature tray landscape).

Moss

Plates 269–274

Figure 75

Like rocks and sand, moss is a vital element in the design of a stone garden. Various miniature landscapes may be made by combining moss with rockwork and garden paths or, by employing moss alone, the garden-maker can depict hills. Moss stays green all year and serves as a decorative ground cover, a kind of grass carpet. It is far superior to other grasses, such as turf, when used in a stone garden.

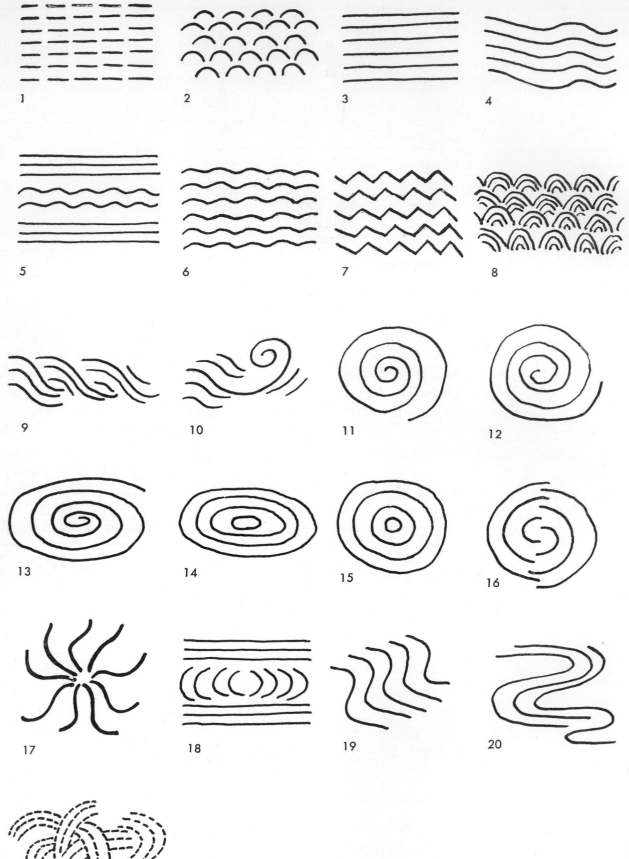

FIG. 74. Types of sand patterns: 1–4) ripplets; 5) snaking stream; 6) swells; 7) triangular waves; 8) jokai-ha; 9) heavy waves; 10–13) whirlpools; 14–16) water rings; 17) lion-figure waves; 18) variation of whirlpool; 19 and 20) running waters; 21) wickerwork-figure waves.

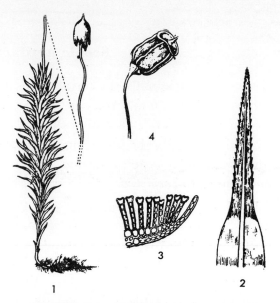

FIG. 75. Hair moss. 1) Full view; 2) detail of leaf; 3) cross section of leaf; 4) seed pod.

Many people think of moss as a plant which grows only on damp ground. This is true only of sphagnum, a type of moss which is not used for stone gardens because it withers when transplanted. The variety used in stone gardens is hair moss *(sugigoke)*. It grows to a height of about 2 inches and more only if it is well cared for. Hair moss grows on rather dry ground. When transplanting takes place, it is set on a pile of nonnutritious red clay earth 6 inches thick. It thrives in a sunny but moderately shady and airy place rather than in a predominantly shady, damp place. Thus it may be planted in yards to the east or south of a building. It will not grow, however, in a place where it does not get adequate moisture, for example under eaves which prevent the ground from catching dew in the night.

It is most important to take good care of the moss during the first year after transplantation. The moss should be weeded carefully and watered at least twice daily, morning and evening. Like the miniature potted trees *(bonsai),* it will need water several times a day in the summer. One should avoid watering in the heat of the day, especially when the moss is exposed to harsh sunlight. In several years the moss will grow thick to a height of about 5 inches. Sometimes the growth chokes the air space, causing the rotting of roots and stems. To prevent this, moss should be raked and the stems separated so that they can get light and air. If the moss is apt to be covered with snow or frost in winter a mulch of pine needles may be used as a protective covering. This should be placed over the moss in the fall rather than in the middle of winter when it has already been covered by frost or snow. Minimum care of hair moss includes keeping it weeded and watered. Well-kept moss develops a gorgeous evergreen quality which increases in beauty with each passing year.

Scenic Artifacts

Plates 275–281
Figures 76, 77 TSUKUBAI: Originally the *tsukubai* was a group of stones used to compose the water basin in a tea garden. It is one of the objects used in the tea ceremony which is also an aesthetic accent in the garden. However, the *tsukubai* may also be placed in a dry landscape or tea garden, as well as in a pond-inlet type of garden. It can be roughly classified into two types: the *muko-bachi tsukubai,* in which the basin is set on the edge of the rockwork arrangement and forms part of the border of the garden (Plate 279), and the *naka-bachi tsukubai,* in which the basin is set in the middle of the rockwork arrangement (Plates 275–278, 280, 281).

Tsukubai literally means "to squat," and this type of stone water basin is installed in a low position. At the *tsukubai* the guest rinses his mouth and washes his hands for physical and spiritual purification. This is an indispensable part of the correctly performed tea ceremony. Quite often today, however, we find the *tsukubai* in many residential gardens. Used thus it adds a clean and calm note to the atmosphere of the garden, functioning as an aesthetic object rather than a practical one. Because of the *tsukubai*'s use in the tea garden it is always placed by the garden path near the entrance to the teahouse. In the stone garden of a residence, however, there is no such restriction. If properly placed, the *tsukubai* enhances the aesthetic effect of the garden by adding to the harmony of the entire composition. Recommended positions for it are near the garden entrance, by the path, or by the entrance to the house. The basin should be positioned where the ground is well drained; it needs clean, flowing water from a piped supply or spring.

Regarding the construction of the *tsukubai,* the standardized form is given in Figures 76 and 77. It is composed of five stone units: a water basin, candle stand, stand for hot water, frontal foot stone, and a drain set. A stone basin of either natural or cut stone may be used for the water basin. The middle part is hewn out, or a stone with a natural depression in the center is used. The candle-stand stone is placed to the left of and set lower than the basin. It is used as a stand for a portable light when the guest washes his hands at night. The stone stand for hot water is on the right side of the basin as the place for a vessel of hot water. The stone is placed lower than the water basin but higher than the candle-stand stone. Since it is uncomfortable in winter to wash one's hands with cold water, the custom of supplying hot water indicates the considerateness of the host. After the water basin itself, the frontal foot stone is the most important of the group. The person using the water stands on this flagstone while he washes his hands. The stone's flat surface is sufficiently large and stable for him to stand comfortably, and its height prevents him from being splashed.

The drain set is made in front of the basin between it and the frontal foot stone. There is a hole in the bottom of this stone which has a natural or man-made depression in it. The water quickly drains through the hole, which is usually covered with round pebbles.

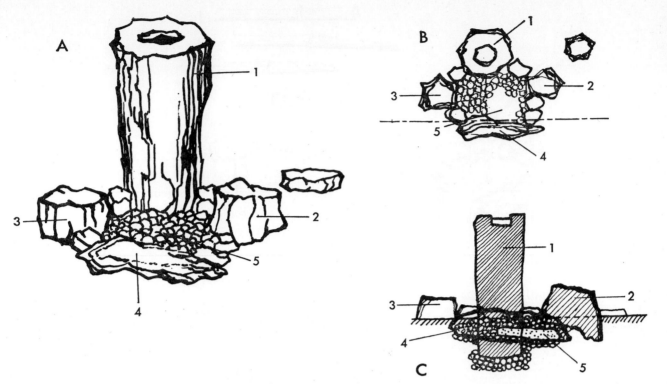

FIG. 76. Tsukubai. A) Front view: 1) water basin; 2) stone for hot water; 3) candle-stand stone; 4) front foot stone; 5) drain set. B) Aerial view. C) Cross-section.

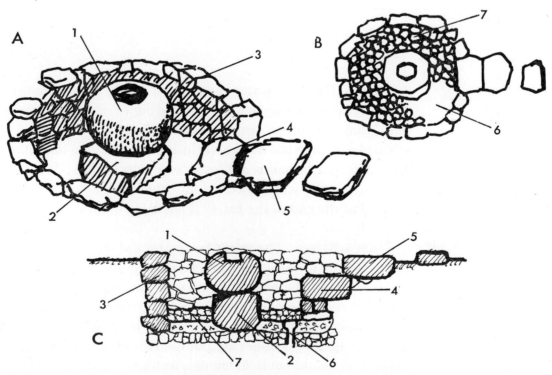

FIG. 77. Ori-tsukubai. This is a variation of the naka-bachi tsukubai. It is located at the bottom of a low area, and the guest steps down to wash his hands. A) View into the ori-tsukubai: 1) water basin; 2) basin-stand rock; 3) embankment; 4–5) front foot stone and steps. B) Aerial view. C) Cross-section: 6) drain set; 7) pebbles.

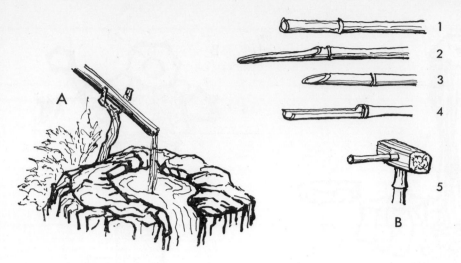

FIG. 78. Water pipes. A) Basic water pipe. B) Variations of the water pipe: 2 and 4) large-mouthed pipes; 1 and 3) small-mouthed pipes; 5) capped water pipe.

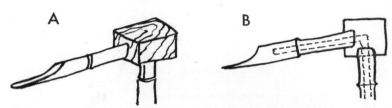

FIG. 79. Kuko wooden caps. A) Basic kuko; B) Cross-section view. The dotted line indicates plastic-tubing placement.

Figures 78, 79   WATER PIPES: A water pipe called *kakehi* brings fresh water to the basin, for the *tsukubai* never uses standing or stagnant water. The pipe is ordinarily made of bamboo with drilled joints. In recent times, however, plastic pipe has been used inside the bamboo one. Bamboo which has been split in half is also used as a water chute. When it is impossible to run the water directly into the basin a wooden piece *(kuko)* is capped at the end of the *kakehi* (Fig. 79).

Plates 282–287   WATER BASINS: The water basin of a *tsukubai* unit may be used independently as a scenic and practical accessory of the garden. It holds clean water in the hollow, ordinarily carried to the basin by pail. In Japan these basins are always installed near a garden shed or toilet where one would want to have water to wash his hands. As a rule, naturally hollowed stones are not used for this type of basin because the depression would not hold enough water to serve several people. A ladle is always placed by the basin. This basin arrangement is composed in the same way as a *tsukubai,* with pebbles around the basin and a drain set at the bottom. In addition to the basin itself, only a frontal foot stone is used. This is an extremely plain composition, even more so than the simplified *tsukubai.*

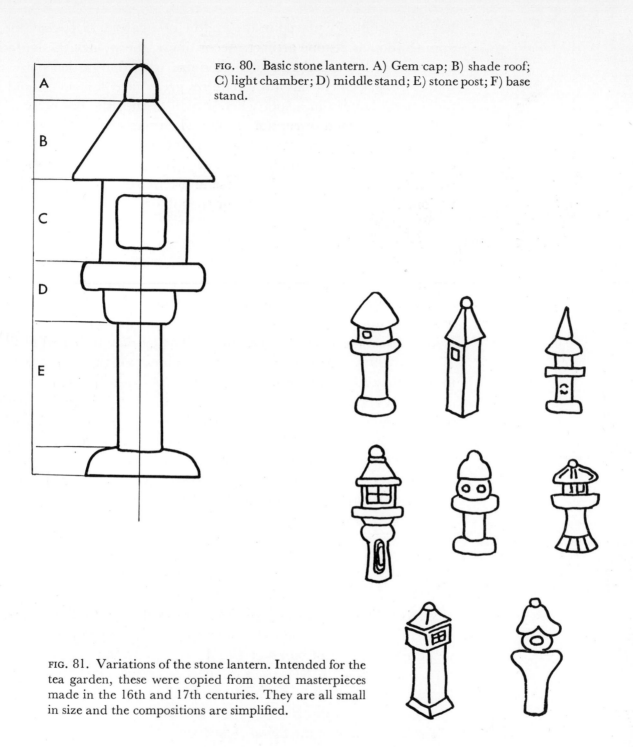

FIG. 80. Basic stone lantern. A) Gem cap; B) shade roof; C) light chamber; D) middle stand; E) stone post; F) base stand.

FIG. 81. Variations of the stone lantern. Intended for the tea garden, these were copied from noted masterpieces made in the 16th and 17th centuries. They are all small in size and the compositions are simplified.

Plates 288–297 STONE LANTERNS: A stone lantern is one of the most favored of all
Figures 80, 81 scenic objects for the garden (see basic forms illustrated in Fig. 81).
It is both a practical and an ornamental piece originally employed to illuminate the garden path. Candle light is used for lanterns today (kerosene lamps were used formerly); electric light should not be used. Paper or glass panes cover the four window openings to keep the light from blowing out, but these are not necessary for a purely ornamental lantern.

Possible placements for a lantern are limited to a turn in the garden path or a junction of paths, but it may also be used to replace the candle-stand stone of a *tsukubai*. The purely ornamental stone lantern, however, is usually placed in the middle of a garden or to one side for appreciation as a stone artifact. Accordingly, the style of the lantern is a simplified form designed to harmonize with the garden's size and shape. Its placement naturally requires great care, for one should not put a stone lantern in a spot where it will disrupt the harmony of the surroundings. Such disruption occurs when one uses a lantern in bad taste, for example, one shaped like a giant mushroom which is added only for appearance without regard to setting. Even in a tea garden, which has a more practical purpose and requires some kind of illumination, the lantern should be no greater than 40 inches in height.

Plates 298, 299   KYOKUSUI: The *kyokusui,* a winding stream, is a possibility which may be included in a stone garden. It was originally developed by nobles and men of letters in ancient China, who held banquets near one. The guests sat along the stream singing, reciting poems, and exchanging drinking cups. Trays of food and liquors from the kitchen area were floated down the *kyokusui* to the guests. The garden presented in Plates 298 and 299 is a modern version of a Chinese pleasure garden of the first century A.D. The central concrete square, with the stream winding around, is about $6\frac{1}{2}$ feet on a side. The water is $4\frac{1}{2}$ inches deep at the point of the water supply and about 5 inches deep at the point where the water is drained off. This produces an incline of only $\frac{1}{2}$ inch from the beginning to the end of the stream. The width of the straight part of the waterway is $6\frac{1}{4}$ inches and $5\frac{3}{8}$ inches at the bend, and the total length of the stream is about 33 feet. From the above description one can imagine how slowly the water will flow.

bonsai: miniature tree
bonseki: miniature stone landscape laid on a tray

double-linked strike: double-stone unit of different-sized stones spaced equidistantly

enzan-seki: symbolic stone or stone arrangement which represents the shape of a noted mountain

fumi-ishi: large flat stone used singly in a path
funa-ishi: boat stone

haku-un-seki: symbolic stone that expresses a white cloud
hashizoe-ishi: attendant rocks at the ends of a stone bridge
hikae-ishi: attendant stone to steppingstones

ikebana: the art of flower arrangement
in: shade element as opposed to *yo*
itokake-ishi: "thread-strung" rock
itsutsu-gusoku: the five essentials of Buddhism: benevolence, justice, courtesy, intelligence, and confidence

jinko-seki: incense stone
jokai-ha: serene waters

kakehi: a water pipe
Kannon-*seki:* rock of the deity of mercy
karataki: dry waterfall symbolized by upright rocks
karataki-ishi: master rock in a karataki rockwork to simulate a waterfall (same as *taki-ishi*)
karesansui: dry landscape garden
kazan: garden built with rocks depicting mountains
kazan-jukei: *shukkei* garden with a collection of condensed scenes or landscapes
kei-seki: symbolic stone or stone arrangement which expresses scenery in a condensed form
kotoji: the bridge of a *koto,* or Japanese harp
kuko: wooden box capped at the elbow of a *kakehi* to hide the bend
kuzan-hakkai: nine mountains and eight seas; *see* Shumisen
kyokusui: winding stream

mei-seki: rare rocks of high value
mittsu-gusoku: three essentials of Buddhism: heaven, earth, man
mizuwake-ishi: "water-dividing" stone
monomi-ishi: lookout stone
muko-bachi tsukubai: rock arrangement with a *tsukubai* at the facing edge

naka-bachi tsukubai: rock arrangement with a *tsukubai* in the middle
nobedan: loosely inlaid stone pavement

"one-foot" stone: stone large enough to accommodate one man's foot
ori-tsukubai: a variation of the *naka-bachi tsukubai*

sabi: the concept of an elegant appearance in age, rusticity, or antiquity
sado: tea cult
san-en: three distant landscapes, a technique of *sumi-e*
sanzan-jisshu: three gigantic mountains and ten vast seas
sanzon-seki: triplet-rock arrangement of Buddhist images
sawa-ishi: valley rock; generally produced in the rapids of a river or by the branch
of a valley stream
sawa-watari: marsh steppingstones
sekko: small stone garden up to six by nine feet in area
sennin: demigod-hermits with supernatural powers
shakkei: borrowed scenery or background
shibui: quiet, tasteful, refined
shiki-ishi: compactly inlaid stone pavement
shoin-style garden: garden constructed facing a living room of a residence or temple
shukkei: miniature landscape created with rockwork and plants
Shumisen: the fantasy world of Buddhism; employs mountains surrounded by seas;
also called *kuzan-hakkai*
sozu: bamboo water-device balanced on a pivot; makes an intermittent clacking
sound when emptying itself
strike: arrangement or arranging of steppingstones
sugigoke: hair moss
sui-seki: water stone
sumi-e: Chinese ink painting in black and white

taiko-bashi: drum-shaped bridge
taki-ishi: master rock in a karataki rockwork (same as *karataki-ishi*)
takitsubo-ishi: basin stones of a waterfall
takizoe-ishi: attendant rocks in a waterfall (same as *wakiji-ishi*)
tora-ishi: tiger rock
triple-linked strike: triple-stone unit of two stones of similar size and one stone of different size
tsukubai: water basin
"two-foot" stone: stone large enough to accommodate a man's two feet

vigor (of a rock): the direction of ridges and lines in a rock's appearance

wakiji-ishi: attendant rocks in a waterfall (same as *takizoe-ishi*)

yaku-ishi: functional stones
yamato-e: the national school of painting developed in the Heian period using purely
Japanese subject matter
yo: light element as opposed to *in*
yoroi-ishi: armor rock

■ Bibliography

BOOKS IN ENGLISH:

Engel, David H.: *Japanese Gardens for Today,* Charles E. Tuttle Company, Tokyo, 1958

Kuck, Loraine: *The World of the Japanese Garden,* John Weatherhill, Inc., Tokyo, 1968

Takakuwa, Gisei and Asano, Giichi: *Invitation to Japanese Gardens,* Charles E. Tuttle Company, Tokyo, 1970

BOOKS IN JAPANESE:

Hishikawa, Moronobu: *Yokei Sakutei no Zu,* Collection of Tokyo College of Agriculture Library, Tokyo, 1680

Kitagawa, Enkinsai: *Tsukiyama-Teizo-den,* 3 vols., Collection of Tokyo College of Agriculture Library, Tokyo, 1735

Mori, Osamu: *Nihon no Teien,* Sogensha, Tokyo, 1958

Rijima-ken, Akizato: *Miyako Rinsen Meisho Zue,* 10 vols., Collection of Tokyo College of Agriculture Library, Tokyo, 1799

Shigemori, Kanto: *Nihon no Teien Geijutsu,* 3 vols., Riko Tosho, Tokyo, 1958

Shigemori, Mirei: *Nihon Teien-shi Zukan,* 26 vols., Ukosha, Tokyo, 1939

————: *Niwa,* Heibonsha, Tokyo, 1964

Yoshimura, Iwao: *Nihon Teien,* Asakura Shoten, Tokyo, 1959

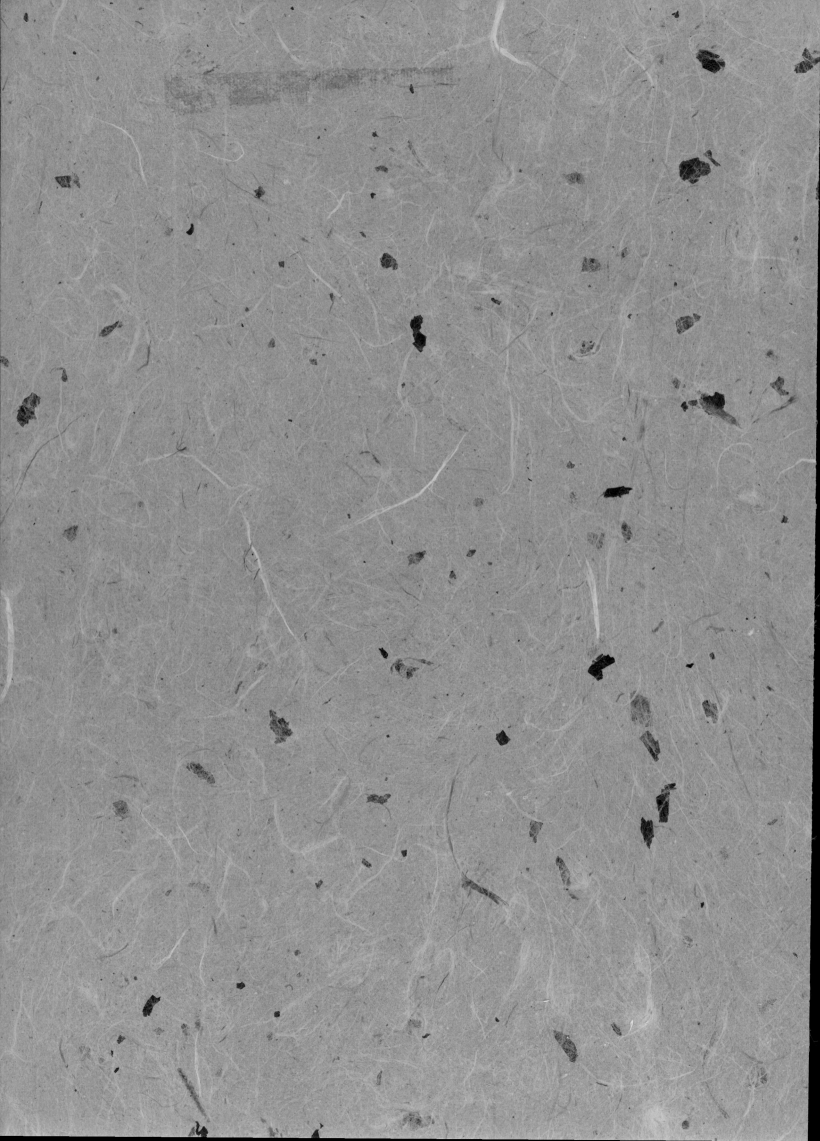